The Church

A
Bibliography

The Church

A
Bibliography

Avery Dulles
&
Patrick Granfield

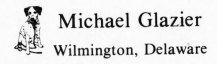 Michael Glazier
Wilmington, Delaware

BIOGRAPHICAL NOTES

Avery Dulles, S.J., has been a professor of systematic theology at The Catholic University of America since 1974. He earned his S.T.D. from the Gregorian University in Rome in 1960, and then taught at Woodstock College, a Jesuit theologate, until 1974. In 1975-76 he served as President of the Catholic Theological Society of America, and in 1978-79 as President of the American Theological Society.

Patrick Granfield, O.S.B., is a professor of systematic theology at The Catholic University of America. He earned his Ph.D. in philosophy from the Anselmianum in Rome in 1958, and his S.T.D. from The Catholic University of America in 1962. He is President of the Catholic Theological Society of America (1984-85).

First published in 1985 by Michael Glazier, Inc., 1723 Delaware Avenue, Wilmington, DE 19806.

Library of Congress Catalog Card Number 84-48453
International Standard Book Number:
The Church: A Bibliography: 0-89453-449-1

Typography by Susan Pickett

Cover design by Florence Bern

Printed in the United States of America

*Dedicated
to
David J. Gilson
R. Bruce Miller
Carolyn Lee
Librarians at
Catholic University of America
For their help throughout the years*

TABLE OF CONTENTS

Introduction

Ecclesiology, as a formal discipline, is a fairly recent arrival on the theological scene. Although there is an abundance of inspiring and valuable material about the Church in the Scriptures, in the Fathers, and in the writings of the Scholastics, these sources provide no systematic treatise on the Church. The *Summa Theologiae* of St. Thomas, for example, does not have a separate treatment of ecclesiology. In the late Middle Ages several important works were written on the relation between the spiritual and the secular power — especially between the papacy and the Empire. One of the first formal studies of the theology of the Church is the *Summa de Ecclesia* by Johannes de Turrecremata (1388-1468) — a work that has been described as built "like the Jewish temple after the Exile, with sword in hand." During the period of the Reformation and Counter-Reformation, there were many ecclesiological texts and most were characterized by a strong controversialist tone. Down through the nineteenth century, the Church was analyzed and defended by theologians who argued polemically and juridically, concentrating more on the external aspects of the Church than on its internal spirit.

A significant change took place in the twentieth century, which the Lutheran theologian, Otto Dibelius, called the "century of the Church." Using material that was emerging from significant scriptural, patristic, historical, and liturgical research, theologians began to develop a richer and more balanced ecclesiology. They realized that ecclesiology is pivotal for the full understanding of how God works in the world through Christ and His Spirit.

The Second Vatican Council (1962-1965) made the Church the principal object of attention and in so doing contributed immensely to the revitalization of ecclesiology. It showed the importance of retrieving the sacramental, pastoral, and ecumenical dimensions of the Church, as well as the relationship between the Church on earth and the final Kingdom of God. The Council emphasized not only the role of the hierarchy but also the roles of clergy, religious, and laity in the mystery of the Church. In its ecumenical orientation, the Council stressed the common elements and vital links between the Roman Catholic, Orthodox, and Protestant Churches and also viewed positively the salvific elements in non-Christian religions.

One of the results of this exciting renewal of ecclesiology has been the vast amount of published material dealing with the Church. It is becoming increasingly difficult to keep abreast of the many books, monographs, and articles. We all have our "To Be Read" list that, unfortunately, grows faster than we can manage. Professional theologians and other Christians frequently feel overwhelmed as they attempt to discover the most recent works in ecclesiology. Sometimes in our quest for contemporaneity, we overlook the more solid works of earlier generations.

Our aim in compiling this bibliography is to indicate the more important ecclesiological writings. Our catalogue is extensive, but it does not pretend to be exhaustive. Although there is an ecclesial dimension to every aspect of theology, we have, in order to make our task more workable, focused specifically on the nature and mission of the Church itself. We have selected works for their historical value, reliability and utility. The limitation of space has forced us, for the most part, to list only books. Yet many of the books cited have bibliographies containing extensive periodical literature.

In our listing of topics, we have included only those areas that we feel are essential to the subject matter of ecclesiology. Certain topics have been omitted, not because they are unrelated to ecclesiology, but because they are independent treatises. For example, sacraments, liturgy, canon law, and Church and society require their own specialized bibliographies. Missiology and ecumenism are subjects too vast to be treated adequately in these pages.

In order to increase the usefulness of the bibliography, we have given English translations of foreign books whenever available. Our selection of works goes though the year 1984.

The audience for this bibliography includes anyone interested in the theology of the Church. We drew up our list principally with Roman Catholic readers in mind, but we have included much material dealing with other Christian communions. Professional theologians, students, Christian educators, clergy, and concerned laity may approach this book differently, but all will find something helpful for their own special needs.

Many people have helped in preparing this bibliography for publication. We are grateful for the suggestions made by Peter F. Chirico, S.S., Robert B. Eno, S.S., Michael A. Fahey, S.J., John T. Ford, C.S.C., John P. Galvin, Robert L. Kinast, Joseph A. Komonchak, Richard P. McBrien, James H. Provost, Francis A. Sullivan, S.J., and Maurice Vidal, S.S. Special thanks are due to Jeanette le Noir for her word-processing skills.

Finally, we hope that this bibliography on the theology of the Church will prove to be a valuable tool for those who are desirous of learning more about the mystery of the community of disciples, the Body of Christ. The prayer of St. Paul is appropriate:

> If we live by the truth in love, we shall grow in all ways into Christ, who is the head by whom the whole body is fitted and joined together, every part adding its own strength, for each separate part to work according to its function. So the body grows until it has built itself up in love (Ephesians 4:15-16)

We invite our readers to submit to the authors any corrections, suggestions, or additions to the bibliography.

Department of Theology   Avery Dulles, S.J.
Catholic University   Patrick Granfield, O.S.B.
   of America
Washington, D.C. 20064

1
Bibliographies

Congar, Yves M.-J. "Chroniques." In *Sainte Église*, 448-696. Unam Sanctam, no. 41. Paris: Cerf, 1963.

_____. "Bulletin d'ecclésiologie." In *Revue des sciences philosophiques et théologiques*. (Appears about once a year, usually by Yves Congar.)

Dupuy, Bernard-Dominique. "Le mystère de l'Église: bibliographie organisée." *La vie spirituelle* 104 (1961): 70-85.

Ephemerides theologicae lovanienses. (Annual "Elenchus bibliographicus.")

Jossua, Jean-Pierre, and Congar, Yves M.-J. *Theology in the Service of God's People.* Chicago: Priory, 1968. (Bibliography of Congar through 1967.)

Valeske, Ulrich. *Votum Ecclesiae.* Part II, pp. 1-210. Munich: Claudius, 1962.

ATLA (American Theological Library Association) publishes several semi-annual, annual, and retrospective

13

indexes to religious literature which contain extensive listings and book review citations. See especially *Religion Index One: Periodicals*; *Religion Index Two: Multi-Author Works* and *Festschriften*; and *Research in Ministry* — an index of D. Min. projects and theses submitted to ATS schools.

Cerdic (Centre de recherches et de documentation des institutions chrétiennes) of the University of Strasbourg publishes several computerized bibliographies. The following are valuable for ecclesiology: *RIC* (Répertoire bibliographique des institutions chrétiennes) and its *Suppléments*; *Oecuménisme*; *Hommes et Église*; *Recherches institutionnelles*; and *État et religion*.

Other useful sources for bibliographical information are: *Bulletin de théologie ancienne et médiévale*; *Bulletin signalétique* (n.527 — *Sciences religieuses*); *Catholic Periodical and Literature Index* (English language); *Internationale oekumenische Bibliographie*; *Theologische Literaturzeitung*; and *Theologische Revue*.

2
Survey Articles

Lawlor, Francis X. "Church. II. (Theology of)." In *New Catholic Encyclopedia*, vol. 3, 683-693. New York: McGraw-Hill, 1967.

Le Guillou, Marie-Joseph, Rahner, Karl, and Sauras, Emilio. "Church." In *Sacramentum Mundi*, vol. 1, 313-337. New York: Herder & Herder, 1968. Articles of Le Guillou and Rahner reprinted in *Encyclopedia of Theology. The Concise Sacramentum Mundi*, pp. 205-227. New York: Seabury, 1975; Tunbridge Wells: Burns & Oates, 1975.

Lerch, Joseph R. "Ecclesiology." In *New Catholic Encyclopedia*, vol. 5, 34-35. New York: McGraw-Hill, 1967.

The following sources contain much helpful historical and theological information on the Church: *Bibellexikon*; *Catholicisme*; *Dictionnaire d'archéologie et de liturgie*; *Dictionnaire de droit canonique*; *Dictionnaire de la Bible, Supplément*; *Dictionnaire d'histoire et de géographie ecclésiastiques*; *Dictionnaire de théologie catholique*; *Dizionario teologico interdisciplinare*; *Enciclopedia cattolica*; *Enciclopedia de la religion católica*; *Encyclopaedia Britannica*; *Encyclopedic Dictionary of Religion*; *Evangelisches Kirchenlexikon*; *Lexikon für Theologie und Kirche*; *Oxford Dictionary of the Christian Church*; *Realenzyklopädie für protestantische Theologie*; *Reallexikon für Antike und Christentum*; *Die Religion in Geschichte und Gegenwart* (Selections from the 2nd edition; Jaroslav Pelikan, ed. *Twentieth-Century Theology in the Making*. 3 vols. New York: Harper & Row; London: Fontana, 1969-1970); and *Theologische Realenzyklopädie*.

3
Collected Readings

Burns, Patrick J., ed. *Mission and Witness.* Westminster, Md.: Newman, 1965.

Dirkswager, Edward J. Jr., ed. *Readings in the Theology of the Church.* Englewood Cliffs, N.J.: Prentice-Hall, 1970.

Rahner, Hugo, et al. *The Church: Readings in Theology.* Compiled at the Canisianum, Innsbruck. New York: Kenedy, 1963.

4
Festschriften

Bäumer, Remigius, and Dolch, Heimo, eds. *Volk Gottes.*
Festgabe für Josef Höfer. Freiburg: Herder, 1967.

Daniélou, Jean, and Vorgrimler, Herbert, eds. *Sentire Ec-*
clesiam. Festgabe H. Rahner. Freiburg: Herder, 1961.
(Historical Studies.)

Editorial Committee of the *Ephemerides theologicae lovan-*
ienses. Ecclesia a Spiritu Sancto edocta. Mélanges
théologiques à Mgr. Gérard Philips. Gembloux: J.
Duculot, 1970.

Granfield, Patrick, and Jungmann, Josef A., eds. *Kyriakon:*
Festschrift Johannes Quasten. 2 vols. Münster: Aschendorff, 1970.

Hein, Lorenz, ed. *Die Einheit der Kirche: Dimensionen*
ihrer Heiligkeit, Katholizität, und Apostolizität.
Festgabe Peter Meinhold zum 70. Geburtstag. Wies-
baden: Steiner, 1977.

Holböck, Ferdinand, and Sartory, Thomas A., eds. *Mysterium Kirche in der Sicht der theologische Disziplinen*. 2 vols. Salzburg: O. Müller, 1962.

Iserloh, Erwin, and Manns, Peter, eds. *Festgabe Josef Lortz*. 2 vols. Baden-Baden: B. Grimm, 1958.

Klinger, Elmar, and Wittstadt, Klaus, eds. *Glaube im Prozess. Christsein nach dem II. Vatikanum. Für Karl Rahner*. Freiburg: Herder, 1984.

Lührmann, Dieter, and Strecker, Georg, eds. *Kirche. Festschrift für Günther Bornkamm zum 75. Geburtstag*. Tübingen: J.C.B. Mohr, 1980. (Articles by Lutheran scholars, mostly on New Testament.)

Nieman, David, and Schatkin, Margaret, eds. *The Heritage of the Early Church. Essays in Honor of Georges Vasilievich Florovsky*. Rome: Institute of Oriental Studies, 1973.

Reding, Marcel, ed. *Abhandlungen über Theologie und Kirche. Festschrift für Karl Adam*. Düsseldorf: Patmos, 1952.

Schnackenburg, Rudolf, Ernst, Josef, and Wanke, Joachim, eds. *Die Kirche des Anfangs. Festschrift für Heinz Schürmann zum 65. Geburtstag*. Leipzig: St. Benno, 1977.

Schilling, Othmar, ed. *Unio Christianorum. Festschrift Kardinal Jaeger*. Paderborn: Bonifacius, 1962.

Schwaiger, Georg, ed. *Konzil und Papst. Historische Beiträge zur Frage der höchsten Gewalt in der Kirche*.

Festschrift für Hermann Tüchle. Paderborn: F. Schöningh, 1968.

Seckler, Max, ed. *Begegnung der Christen. Festschrift H. Fries.* Graz: Styria, 1972. (Essays on ecumenical themes by Protestants and Catholics.)

Siepen, Karl, Weitzel, Joseph, and Wirth, Paul, eds. *Ecclesia et Ius. Festschrift für Audomar Scheuermann.* Paderborn: F. Schöningh, 1968.

5
Official Roman
Catholic Documents

Congregation for the Doctrine of the Faith. *Mysterium ecclesiae*. *Acta Apostolicae Sedis* 65 (1973): 396-408. English translation: "Declaration in Defense of the Catholic Doctrine on the Church against Certain Errors of the Present." *Catholic Mind* 71 (1973): 54-64.

Gremillion, Joseph, ed. *The Gospel of Peace and Justice: Catholic Social Teaching since Pope John.* Maryknoll, N.Y.: Orbis, 1976.

John Paul II. *Redemptor hominis. Acta Apostolicae Sedis* 71 (1979): 257-324. English translation: *The Papal Encyclicals 1958-1981*, pp. 245-273. Edited by Claudia Carlen. Wilmington, N.C.: McGrath, 1981.

Leo XIII. *Satis cognitum. Acta Sanctae Sedis* 28 (1895-1896): 708-739. English translation: *The Papal Encyclicals 1878-1903*, pp. 387-404. Edited by Claudia Carlen. Wilmington, N.C.: McGrath, 1981.

Meyer, Harding, and Vischer, Lukas, eds. *Growth in Agreement. Reports and Agreed Statements of Ecumenical Conversations on a World Level.* Ecumenical Documents II. New York: Paulist; Geneva: World Council of Churches, 1984.

O'Brien, David J., and Shannon, Thomas A., eds. *Renewing the Earth: Catholic Documents on Peace, Justice and Liberation.* Garden City, N.Y.: Doubleday Image, 1977; London: Doubleday & Co., 1977.

Papal Teachings: The Church. Selected and arranged by the Benedictine Monks of Solesmes. Boston: St. Paul, 1962.

Paul VI. *Ecclesiam suam. Acta Apostolicae Sedis* 56 (1964): 609-659. English translation: *The Papal Encyclicals 1958-1981,* pp. 135-160. Edited by Claudia Carlen. Wilmington, N.C.: McGrath, 1981.

_____. *Evangelii nuntiandi. Acta Apostolicae Sedis* 68 (1976): 5-76. English translation: *Evangelization in the Modern World.* Washington, D.C.: USCC, 1976.

Pius XII. *Mystici corporis. Acta Apostolicae Sedis* 35 (1943): 193-248. English translation: *The Papal Encyclicals 1939-1958,* pp. 35-63. Edited by Claudia Carlen. Wilmington, N.C.: McGrath, 1981.

Stransky, Thomas F., and Sheerin, John B., eds. *Doing Truth in Charity.* Statements of Pope Paul VI, Popes John Paul I, John Paul II, and the Secretariat for Promoting Christian Unity 1964-1980. Ecumenical Documents I. New York: Paulist, 1982.

Synod of Bishops (1971). *The Ministerial Priesthood and Justice in the World.* Washington, D.C.: NCCB, 1971.

Vatican Council I. *Supremi pastoris (Prima schema constitutionis de ecclesia Christi).* Latin text in *Sacrorum conciliorum nova et amplissima collectio*, vol. 51, 539-553. Edited by J. D. Mansi. Florence, 1759ff; Paris-Leipzig, 1901-1927. Partial English translation in *The Church Teaches*, pp. 87-94. Edited by J. F. Clarkson et al. St. Louis: B. Herder, 1955.

_____. *Tametsi Deus (Schema constitutionis dogmaticae secundae de ecclesia Christi).* Prepared by Joseph Kleutgen. The Latin text and the *Relatio* by Kleutgen in *Sacrorum conciliorum nova et amplissima collectio*, vol. 53, 308-332. Edited by J. D. Mansi. Florence, 1759ff; Paris-Leipzig, 1901-1927.

_____. *Pastor aeternus (Constitutio dogmatica de ecclesia Christi).* Latin text in *Sacrorum conciliorum nova et amplissima collectio*, vol. 52:1330-1334. Edited by J. D. Mansi. Florence, 1759ff; Paris-Leipzig, 1901-1927. English translation with Latin text can be found in *Dublin Review* 67 (1870): 496-507.

Vatican Council II. *Acta et documenta concilio oecumenico Vaticano II apparando. Series I (Antepraeparatoria).* Vatican City: Typis Polyglottis Vaticanis, 1960-1961.

_____. *Acta et documenta concilio oecumenico Vaticano II apparando. Series II (Praeparatoria).* Vatican City: Typis Polyglottis Vaticanis, 1964-1969.

_____. *Acta synodalia sacrosancti concilii oecumenici Vatican II.* Vatican City: Typis Polyglottis Vaticanis, 1970-1980.

_____. *Sacrosanctum oecumenicum concilium Vaticanum II: Constitutiones, decreta, declarationes.* Vatican City: Typis Polyglottis Vaticanis, 1966.

_____. *Ad gentes. Decree on the Missionary Activity of the Church. Vatican Council II: The Conciliar and Post-Conciliar Documents.* pp. 813-856. Edited by Austin Flannery. Northport, New York: Costello, 1975; Dublin: Dominican, 1975.

_____. *Gaudium et spes. Pastoral Constitution on the Church in the Modern World. Vatican Council II: Conciliar and Post-Conciliar Documents.* pp. 903-1001. Edited by Austin Flannery. Northport, New York: Costello, 1975; Dublin, Dominican, 1975.

_____. *Lumen gentium. Dogmatic Constitution on the Church. Vatican Council II: The Conciliar and Post-Conciliar Documents.* pp. 350-432. Edited by Austin Flannery. Northport, New York: Costello, 1975; Dublin, Dominican, 1975.

_____. *Unitatis redintegratio. Decree on Ecumenism. Vatican Council II: The Conciliar and Post-Conciliar Documents.* pp. 452-472. Edited by Austin Flannery. Northport, New York: Costello, 1975; Dublin, Dominican, 1975.

6
Classics of Ecclesiology

The following list is restricted to works published before 1930.

Adam, Karl. *The Spirit of Catholicism*. Revised edition. New York: Macmillan, 1929.

Bellarminus, Robertus. *De controversiis christianae fidei*. In *Opera omnia*, 12 vols. Edited by Justinus Fèvre. Paris: L. Vivès, 1870-1874.

Billot, Ludovicus. *De ecclesia Christi*. 5th edition. Rome: Gregoriana, 1927.

Capocci, Giacomo (James of Viterbo). *Le plus ancien traité de l'Église: Jacques de Viterbe, De regimine christiano*. Edited by H.-X. Arquillière. Paris: Beauchesne, 1926.

Colonna, Egidio (Giles of Rome). *De ecclesiastica potestate*. Weimar: Böhnaus, 1929.

Franzelin, Johannes B. *Theses de ecclesia Christi*. Rome: Ex Typographia Polyglotta S.C. de Propaganda Fide, 1887. 2nd edition, 1907.

Jean (Quidort) de Paris. *De potestate regia et papali.* Text reproduced in Jean Leclercq. *Jean de Paris et l'ecclésiologie au XIIIe siècle.* Paris: J. Vrin, 1942. English version: *On Royal and Papal Power.* Translation with introduction by Arthur P. Monahan, New York: Columbia University, 1974.

Möhler, Johann Adam. *Die Einheit in der Kirche: oder, Das Prinzip des Katholicismus.* New edition. Edited by J. R. Geiselmann. Cologne: Hegner, 1957. (French translation: *L'unité dans l'Église.* Unam Sanctam, no. 2. Paris: Cerf, 1938.)

Passaglia, Carlo. *De ecclesia Christi.* 2 vols. Regensburg: G. J. Manz, 1853-1856.

Schrader, Clemens. *De unitate Romana.* Freiburg: Herder, 1862.

Turrecremata, Johannes de. *Summa de ecclesia.* Rome: 1489; Venice: Apud M. Tramenzinum, 1561.

7
History of Ecclesiology

*Bouyer, Louis. *The Church of God: Body of Christ and Temple of the Holy Spirit*, pp. 3-155. Chicago: Franciscan Herald, 1982.

*Congar, Yves M.-J. *L'ecclésiologie de S. Augustin à l'époque moderne*. Paris: Cerf, 1970. This is a French version of his contribution to *Handbuch der Dogmengeschichte* (see below).

Gratsch, Edward J. *Where Peter Is: A Survey of Ecclesiology*. Staten Island, N.Y.: Alba House, 1975.

Handbuch der Dogmengeschichte. Vol. 3, fascicles a-d. "Die Lehre von der Kirche." By P. V. Dias, P. T. Camelot, and Y. M.-J. Congar. Freiburg: Herder, 1970-1974.

Jay, Eric G. *The Church: Its Changing Image Through Twenty Centuries*. Atlanta: J. Knox, 1980. Volume 1. *The First Seventeen Centuries*. London: SPCK, 1977. Volume 2: *1700 to the Present Day*. London: SPCK, 1978.

*An asterisk before a title indicates that the work is of broad interest and serves as a good introduction to the topic.

8
New Testament

Banks, Robert J. *Paul's Idea of Community.* Grand Rapids: W. B. Eerdmans, 1980; Exeter: Paternoster Press, 1981.

Benoit, Pierre. *Exégèse et théologie.* 3 vols. Paris: Cerf, 1961-1968.

Brown, Raymond E. *Biblical Reflections on Crises Facing the Church.* New York: Paulist, 1975; London: Darton, Longman & Todd, 1975.

_____. *The Churches the Apostles Left Behind.* New York: Paulist, 1984.

_____. *The Community of the Beloved Disciple.* New York: Paulist, 1979; London: G. Chapman, 1979.

_____. *Priest and Bishop: Biblical Reflections.* New York: Paulist, 1970.

Brown, Raymond E., Donfried, Karl P., and Reumann, John, eds. *Peter in the New Testament.* Minneapolis: Augsburg; New York: Paulist, 1973; London: G. Chapman, 1974.

Brown, Raymond E., and Meier, John P. *Antioch and Rome: New Testament Cradles of Catholic Christianity.* New York: Paulist, 1983; London: C. Chapman, 1983.

Bourke, Myles M. "Reflections on Church Order in the New Testament." *Catholic Biblical Quarterly* 30 (1968): 493-511.

Campenhausen, Hans von. *Ecclesiastical Authority and Spiritual Power in the Church of the First Three Centuries.* Stanford, CA: Stanford University, 1969.

Cerfaux, Lucien. *The Church in the Theology of St. Paul.* New York: Herder & Herder, 1959.

Cody, Aelred. "The Foundation of the Church: Biblical Criticism for Ecumenical Discussion." *Theological Studies* 34 (1973): 3-18.

Cullmann, Oscar. *Peter: Disciple, Apostle, Martyr.* London: SCM, 1961.

_____. *The State in the New Testament.* New York: Scribners, 1956.

Davies, John G. *The Early Christian Church.* New York: Holt, Rinehart and Winston, 1965; London: Greenwood Press, 1977.

Dunn, James D. G. *Unity and Diversity in the New Testament.* Philadelphia: Westminster, 1977; London, SCM, 1981.

Fiorenza, Francis S. *Foundational Theology: Jesus and the Church,* chapters 3-6. New York: Crossroad, 1984.

Gager, John G. *Kingdom and Community: The Social World of Early Christianity.* Englewood Cliffs, N.J.: Prentice-Hall, 1975.

Giblet, Jean, et al. *The Birth of the Church.* Staten Island, N.Y.: Alba House, 1968.

Guitton, Jean. *The Church and the Gospel.* Westminster, Md.: Newman, 1961.

Harrington, Daniel J. *God's People in Christ: New Testament Perspectives on the Church and Judaism.* Philadelphia: Fortress, 1980.

Hoffmann, Joseph. "L'Église et son origine." In *Initiation à la pratique de la théologie*, vol. 3, 55-141. Edited by B. Lauret and F. Refoulé. Paris: Cerf, 1983.

Holmberg, Bengt. *Paul and Power: The Structure of Authority and Power in the Primitive Church as Reflected in the Pauline Epistles.* Philadelphia: Fortress, 1980.

Karrer, Otto. *Peter and the Church: An Examination of Cullmann's Thesis.* New York: Herder & Herder, 1963.

Käsemann, Ernst. *Essays on New Testament Themes.* Naperville, Ill.: Allenson; London: SCM, 1964.

_____. *New Testament Questions for Today.* Philadelphia: Fortress, 1963; London: SCM, 1969.

Kelber, Werner H. *The Oral and the Written Gospel.* Philadelphia: Fortress, 1983.

Knox, John. *The Early Church and the Coming Great Church*. New York: Abingdon, 1955.

Lohfink, Gerhard. *Jesus and Community: The Social Dimension of Christian Faith*. New York: Paulist; Philadelphia: Fortress, 1984.

Lohse, Eduard. *The First Christians: Their Beginnings, Writings, and Beliefs*. Philadelphia: Fortress, 1983.

Malherbe, Abraham. *Social Aspects of Early Christianity*. Baton Rouge: Louisiana State University, 1977.

Martin, Ralph P. *The Family and the Fellowship: New Testament Images of the Church*. Grand Rapids: W. B. Eerdmans, 1980; Exeter: Paternoster Press, 1980.

Meeks, Wayne, A. *The First Urban Christians*. New Haven: Yale University, 1983.

McKelvey, R. J. *The New Temple: The Church in the New Testament*. London: Oxford, 1969.

Minear, Paul S. *Images of the Church in the New Testament*. Philadelphia: Westminster, 1960.

Schlier, Heinrich. *Die Zeit der Kirche: Exegetische Aufsätze und Vorträge*. Freiburg: Herder, 1962.

_____. "Ekklesiologie des Neuen Testaments." In *Mysterium salutis*, vol. IV/1, 101-221. Edited by Johannes Feiner and Magnus Löhrer. Einsiedeln: Benziger, 1972. (Extensive bibliography.)

Schmidt, Karl L. *The Church. Bible Key Words from Kittel.* New York: Harper, 1951.

*Schnackenburg, Rudolf. *The Church in the New Testament.* New York: Herder & Herder, 1965.

_____. *God's Rule and Kingdom.* New York: Herder & Herder, 1963.

Schweizer, Eduard. *Church Order in the New Testament.* Naperville, Ill.: Allenson, 1961; London: SCM, 1979.

Senior, Donald, and Stuhlmueller, Carroll. *The Biblical Foundations for Mission.* Maryknoll, N.Y.: Orbis, 1983; SCM, 1983.

Stanley, David M. *The Apostolic Church in the New Testament.* Westminster, Md.: Newman, 1965.

Stendahl, Krister. "Kirche, II. Im Urchristentum." *Religion in Geschichte und Gegenwart.* Third edition. Vol. 1, col. 1279-1304. Tübingen: J. C. B. Mohr, 1959.

Theissen, Gerd. *Sociology of Early Christianity.* Philadelphia: Fortress, 1977; London: SCM, 1978.

Verbraken, Patrick. *The Beginnings of the Church.* Glen Rock, N.J.: Paulist, 1968.

*Warnach, Viktor. "Church." In *Sacramentum Verbi.* Vol. 1, 101-116. New York: Herder & Herder, 1970.

Zehnle, Richard. *The Making of the Christian Church.* Notre Dame, Ind.: Fides, 1969.

9
The Patristic Era

Bardy, Gustave. *La théologie de l'Église, de S. Clément de Rome à S. Irénée.* Unam Sanctam, no. 13. Paris: Cerf, 1945.

_____. *La théologie de l'Église, de S. Irénée au Concile de Nicée.* Unam Sanctam, no. 14. Paris: Cerf, 1947.

Campenhausen, Hans von. *Ecclesiastical Authority and Spiritual Power in the Church of the First Three Centuries.* Stanford, CA: Stanford University, 1969.

Colson, Jean. *Les fonctions ecclésiales aux deux premiers siècles.* Paris: Desclée De Brouwer, 1965.

Daniélou, Jean, and Vorgrimler, Herbert, eds. *Sentire Ecclesiam. Festgabe H. Rahner.* Freiburg: Herder, 1961. (Historical studies.)

Delahaye, Karl. *Ecclesia Mater chez les Pères des trois premiers siècles.* Unam Sanctam, no. 46. Paris: Cerf, 1964.

*Evans, Robert F. *One and Holy: The Church in Latin Patristic Thought.* London: SPCK, 1972.

Fuellenbach, John. *Ecclesiastical Office and the Primacy of Rome. An Evaluation of Recent Theological Discussion of First Clement.* Washington, D.C.: Catholic University of America, 1980.

*Hertling, Ludwig. *Communio: Church and Papacy in Early Christianity.* Introduction by Jared Wicks. Chicago: Loyola University, 1972.

Ladner, Gerhart B. *The Idea of Reform: Its Impact on Christian Thought and Action in the Age of the Fathers.* Cambridge, Mass.: Harvard University, 1959.

Mersch, Émile. *The Whole Christ: The Historical Development of the Doctrine of the Mystical Body.* Milwaukee: Bruce, 1938; Durham: Dobson Books, 1949.

Plumpe, Joseph C. *Mater Ecclesia: An Inquiry into the Concept of the Church as Mother in Early Christianity.* Washington, D.C.: Catholic University of America, 1943.

Rahner, Hugo. *Symbole der Kirche: Die Ekklesiologie der Väter.* Salzburg: Müller, 1964.

Scazzoso, Piero. *Introduzione alla ecclesiologia di S. Basilio.* Milan: Università Cattolica del S. Cuore, 1975.

10
St. Augustine

The works given here are in addition to the items referred to in the preceeding section.

Balthasar, Hans Urs von. *Augustinus, Das Antlitz der Kirche.* Einsiedeln: Benziger, 1955. (French translation: *S. Augustin: Le visage de l'Église: textes choisis et présentés.* Unam Sanctam, no. 31. Paris: Cerf, 1958.)

Borgomeo, Pasquale. *L'Église de ce temps dans la prédication de St. Augustin.* Paris: Études Augustiniennes, 1972.

*Grabowski, Stanislaus J. *The Church: An Introduction to the Theology of St. Augustine.* St. Louis: Herder, 1957.

Hofmann, Fritz. *Der Kirchenbegriff des hl. Augustinus.* Munich: M. Hueber, 1933. Reprinted Münster: Th. Stenderhoff, 1978.

Lamirande, Émilien. *Études sur l'ecclésiologie de S. Augustin.* Ottawa: Université Saint-Paul et Université d'Ottawa, 1969.

_____. *La situation ecclésiologique des Donatistes d'après S. Augustin.* Ottawa: Université d'Ottawa, 1972.

_____. "Un siècle et demi d'études sur l'ecclésiologie de saint Augustin." *Revue des études Augustiniennes* 8 (1962): 1-125. (A bibliography from 1809 to 1954.)

Ratzinger, Joseph. "Die Kirche in der Frömmigkeit des heiligen Augustinus." In *Sentire Ecclesiam. Festgabe H. Rahner*, pp. 152-175. Edited by Jean Daniélou and Herbert Vorgrimler. Freiburg: Herder, 1961.

_____. *Volk und Haus Gottes in Augustins Lehre von der Kirche.* Munich: Zink, 1954.

11
The Middle Ages

Alberigo, Giuseppe. *Cardinalato e Collegialità*. Florence: Vallecchi, 1969.

_____. *Chiesa conciliare. Identità e significato del conciliarismo*. Brescia: Paideia, 1981.

Black, Antony. *Council and Commune. The Conciliar Movement and the Council of Basle*. London: Burns & Oates; Shepherdstown, W. Va.: Patmos, 1979.

_____. "What Was Conciliarism? Conciliar Theory in Historical Perspective." In *Authority and Power: Studies in Medieval Law and Government*, pp. 213-224. Edited by Brian Tierney and Peter Linehan. Cambridge, Eng.: Cambridge University, 1980.

Congar, Yves M.-J. "Ecclesia ab Abel," in *Abhandlungen über Theologie und Kirche. Festschrift für Karl Adam*. Edited by Marcel Reding. Düsseldorf: Patmos, 1952.

_____. *L'ecclésiologie du haut moyen-âge, de S. Grégoire le Grand à la désunion entre Byzance et Rome*. Paris: Cerf, 1968.

*—————. *L'Église de S. Augustin à l'époque moderne.*
Paris: Cerf, 1970.

Delaruelle, Étienne, et al. *L'Église au temps du Grand
Schisme et de la crise conciliaire.* In *Histoire
de l'Église*, vol. 14. Edited by Fliche-Martin.
Paris: 1952.

Franzen, August. "The Council of Constance." Concilium,
no. 7, 29-68. Edited by Roger Aubert. Glen Rock,
N.J.: Paulist, 1965.

Huss, John *Tractatus de Ecclesia.* English version: *The
Church by John Huss.* Translation by David S.
Schaff. Westport, Conn.: Greenwood, 1971). (Reprint
from N.Y.: C. Scribner's Sons, 1915.)

Izbicki, Thomas M. *Protector of the Faith: Johannes de
Turrecremata and the Defense of the Institutional
Church.* Washington, D.C.: Catholic University of
America, 1981.

*Küng, Hans. *Structures of the Church.* pp. 268-319. New
York: T. Nelson, 1964. (Discussion of conciliarism.)

Lecler, Joseph. *Le pape ou le concile? Une interrogation
de l'Église médiévale.* Lyon: Le Chalet, 1973.

Leclercq, Jean. *Jean de Paris et l'ecclésiologie au XIIIe
siècle.* Paris: J. Vrin, 1942.

Lytle, Guy F., ed. *Reform and Authority in the Medieval
and Reformation Church.* Washington, D.C.: Catholic University of America, 1981.

Oakley, Francis. *Council over Pope? Towards a Provisional
Ecclesiology.* New York: Herder & Herder, 1969.

_____. "The 'New Conciliarism' and Its Implications: A Problem of History and Hermeneutics." *Journal of Ecumenical Studies* 8 (1971): 815-840.

Pascoe, Louis B. *Jean Gerson: Principles of Church Reform.* Leiden: Brill, 1973.

Ryan, John J. *The Nature, Structure and Function of the Church in William of Ockham.* American Academy of Religion, Studies in Religion, no. 16. Missoula, Mont.: Scholars Press, 1979.

Spinka, Matthew. *John Hus' Concept of the Church.* Princeton, N.J.: Princeton University, 1966.

*Tierney, Brian. *Foundations of Conciliar Theory: The Contributions of the Medieval Canonists from Gratian to the Great Schism.* Cambridge, Eng.: Cambridge University, 1955.

_____. *The Origins of Papal Infallibility (1150-1350).* Leiden: Brill, 1973.

Ullmann, Walter. *The Growth of Papal Government in the Middle Ages.* London: Methuen, 1955.

Vooght, Paul de. *Les pouvoirs du concile et l'autorité du pape au concile de Constance.* Unam Sanctam, no. 56. Paris: Cerf, 1965.

_____. "The Results of Recent Historical Research on Conciliarism." In *Papal Ministry in the Church*, 148-157. Edited by Hans Küng. Concilium, no. 64. New York: Herder & Herder, 1971.

12
St. Thomas Aquinas

The following material on St. Thomas is in addition to the references given in the previous section on the Middle Ages.

Congar, Yves M.-J. "The Idea of the Church in St. Thomas Aquinas." In *The Mystery of the Church*, chapter 3. Baltimore: Helicon, 1960.

*Dulles, Avery. "The Church according to Thomas Aquinas." In *A Church to Believe In*, chapter 10. New York: Crossroad, 1982.

Grabmann, Martin. *Die Lehre des hl. Thomas von Aquin von der Kirche als Gotteswerk*. Regensburg: G. J. Manz, 1903.

Ménard, Étienne. *La Tradition: révélation, écriture, Église selon S. Thomas d'Aquin*. Paris: Desclée De Brouwer, 1964.

O'Neill, Colman. "St. Thomas on the Membership of the Church." *Vatican II: The Theological Dimension. Thomist* 27 (1963): 88-140.

Seckler, Max. *Das Heil in der Geschichte*. Munich: Kösel, 1964.

13
The Reformation

Avis, Paul D. *The Church in the Theology of the Reformers.* Atlanta: J. Knox, 1981.

Congar, Yves M.-J. *Vraie et fausse Réforme.* Unam Sanctam, no. 20. Paris: Cerf, 1950. (See chapters on the ecclesiology of Luther.)

Ganoczy, Alexandre. *Calvin: Théologien de l'Église et du ministère.* Unam Sanctam, no. 48. Paris: Cerf, 1964.

Gassmann, Benno. *Ecclesia Reformata. Die Kirche in den reformierten Bekentnisschriften.* Freiburg: Herder, 1968.

*Hendrix, Scott H. *Luther and the Papacy: Stages in a Reformation Conflict.* Philadelphia: Fortress, 1981.

Manns, Peter, and Meyer, Harding, eds., in collaboration with Carter Lindberg and Harry McSorley. *Luther's Ecumenical Significance: An Interconfessional Consultation.* Philadelphia: Fortress; New York: Paulist,

1984. (See articles on Luther's ecclesiology by H. Vajta and H.-W. Scheele, pp. 111-158.)

Meyer, Harding, and Schütte, Heinz. "The Concept of the Church in the Augsburg Confession." In *Confessing One Faith: A Joint Commentary on the Augsburg Confession by Lutheran and Catholic Theologians*, pp. 173-201. Edited by George W. Forell and James F. McCue. Minneapolis: Augsburg, 1982.

*Milner, Benjamin C. *Calvin's Doctrine of the Church*. Leiden: Brill, 1970.

Preus, Herman A. *The Communion of Saints: A Study of the Origin and Development of Luther's Doctrine of the Church*. Minneapolis: Augsburg, 1948.

Torrance, Thomas F. *Kingdom and Church: A Study in the Theology of the Reformation*. Edinburgh: Oliver & Boyd, 1956. (On Luther, Butzer, Calvin.)

14
The Seventeenth through the Nineteenth Century

Alberigo, Giuseppe. *Lo sviluppo della dottrina sui poteri nella chiesa universale: momenti essenziali tra il XVI e XIX secolo*. Rome: Herder, 1964.

At, Jean-Antoine. *Les apologistes français au XIXe siècle*. Paris: Bloud et Barral, 1898.

Bárczay, Gyula. *Ecclesia semper reformanda. Eine Untersuchung zum Kirchenbegriff des 19. Jahrhunderts*. Zurich: EVZ, 1969.

Chaillet, Pierre, ed. *L'Église est une: hommage à Möhler*. Paris: Bloud et Gay, 1939.

Costigan, Richard F. *Rohrbacher and the Ecclesiology of Ultramontanism*. Rome: Gregoriana, 1980.

*Facoltà teologica interregionale Milano. *L'ecclesiologia dal Vaticano I al Vaticano II*. Brescia: La Scuola, 1973. (Articles by A. Antón, G. Thils, C. Vagaggini, U. Betti, and others.)

Hardon, John. "Robert Bellarmine's Concept of the Church." In *Studies in Medieval Culture*, vol. 2, 120-127. Edited by J. Sommerfeldt. Western Michigan Press, 1966.

Hocedez, Edgar. *Histoire de la théologie au XIXe siècle.* 3 vols. Brussels: Universelle; Paris: Desclée De Brouwer, 1948.

Martimort, Aimé-Georges. *Le Gallicanisme.* Paris: Presses universitaires de France, 1973.

Martin, Victor. *Les origines du Gallicanisme.* 2 vols. Paris: Bloud et Gay, 1939.

*Nédoncelle, Maurice, Aubert, Roger, Congar, Y. M.-J. et al. *L'ecclésiologie au XIXe siècle.* Unam Sanctam, no. 34. Paris: Cerf, 1960.

Palmer, William. *A Treatise on the Church of Christ.* 2nd ed. 2 vols. New York: Appleton, 1841. (Anglo-Catholic.)

Pottmeyer, Hermann-Josef. *Unfehlbarkeit und Souveränität. Die päpstliche Unfehlbarkeit im System der ultramontanen Ekklesiologie des 19. Jahrhunderts.* Mainz: Matthias-Grünewald, 1975.

Tavard, George H. *The Quest for Catholicity. A Study in Anglicanism,* New York: Herder & Herder, 1964.

Thils, Gustave. *Les notes de l'Église dans l'apologétique catholique depuis la Réforme.* Gembloux: J. Duculot, 1937.

15
Vatican Council I

*Aubert, Roger. "L'ecclésiologie au Concile du Vatican." In *Le Concile et les Conciles*. Chevetogne: Chevetogne, 1960.

_____. *Vatican I*. Paris: Orante, 1964.

Betti, Umberto. *La costituzione dommatica: 'Pastor Aeternus' del Concilio Vaticano I*. Rome: Antonianum, 1961.

*Butler, Cuthbert. *The Vatican Council*. Reissue, Westminster, Md.: Newman, 1962.

Dejaifve, Georges. "First among Bishops." *Eastern Churches Quarterly* 14 (1961): 2-25.

_____. "Ex sese, non autem ex consensu ecclesiae." *Salesianum* 24 (1962): 283-297. Also in *Symposium international de théologie dogmatique fondamentale* (Louvain, 1961). Turin: Società editrice internationale, 1962.

Fessler, J. *The True and False Infallibility of the Popes.*
New York: Catholic Publication Society, 1875.

Granderath, Theodor. *Constitutiones dogmaticae sacro-*
santi oecumenici concilii Vaticani ex ipsis actis expli-
catae atque illustratae. Freiburg: Herder, 1892.

_____. *Geschichte des Vatikanischen Konzils von*
seiner ersten Ankündigung bis seiner Vertragung.
Edited by Konrad Kirch. 3 vols. Freiburg: Herder,
1903-1906. (French version: *Histoire du concile du*
Vatican, depuis sa première annonce jusqu'à sa pro-
rogation. 4 vols. Brussels: A. Dewit, 1907-1914.)

Hasler, August B. *Pius IX (1846-1878), päptsliche Unfehl-*
barkeit, und I. Vatikanisches Konzil: Dogmatisierung
und Durchsetzung einer Ideologie. 2 vols. Stuttgart:
Anton Hiersemann, 1977. (A shorter version in English: *How the Pope Became Infallible: Pius IX and*
the Politics of Persuasion. Garden City, N.J.: Doubleday, 1981; London: Sheldon Press, 1982.)

Hennesey, James. *The First Council of the Vatican: The*
American Experience. New York: Herder & Herder,
1963.

Horst, Fidelis van der. *Das Schema über die Kirche auf dem*
I. Vatikanischen Konzil. Paderborn: Bonifacius,
1963.

Newman, John Henry. "A Letter Addressed to His Grace
the Duke of Norfolk." In *Newman and Gladstone:*
The Vatican Decrees. Edited by A. S. Ryan. Notre
Dame, Ind.: University of Notre Dame, 1962.

Thils, Gustave. *L'infallibilité pontificale: sources, conditions, limites.* Gembloux: J. Duculot, 1969.

_____. *La primauté pontificale. La doctrine de Vatican I.* Gembloux: J. Duculot, 1972.

Torrell, Jean-Pierre. *La théologie de l'épiscopat au premier Concile du Vatican.* Unam Sanctam, no. 37. Paris: Cerf, 1961.

16
Vatican Council II

N.B. The following two books are most useful in working with the Council documents.

Delhaye, Philippe, Guéret, Michel, and Tombeur, Paul, eds. *Concilium Vaticanum II. Concordance, index, listes de fréquence, tables comparatives.* Louvain: Cetedoc, 1974.

Ochoa, Xaverius, ed. *Index verborum cum documentis Concilii Vaticani Secundi.* Rome: Commentarium pro Religiosis, 1967.

• • •

Acerbi, Antonio. *Due ecclesiologie. Ecclesiologia giuridica ed ecclesiologia di communione nella "Lumen gentium."* Bologna: Dehoniane, 1975.

Alberigo, Giuseppe, ed. *L'ecclesiologia del Vaticano II: Dinamismi e prospettive.* Bologna: Dehoniane, 1981. (Articles by G. Alberigo, P. Fransen, H.-J. Pottmeyer, and others.) (French version: *Les Églises après Vatican II. Dynamisme et prospective.* Paris: Beauchesne, 1981.) There is also a German edition.

Alberigo, Giuseppe, and Magistretti, Franca. *Constitutionis dogmaticae Lumen gentium synopsis historica.* Bologna: Istituto per le scienze religiose, 1975.

Baraúna, Guilherme, ed. *L'Église de Vatican II.* 3 vols. Unam Sanctam, no. 51 a, b, and c. Paris: Cerf, 1966. (Italian version: *La Chiesa del Vaticano II.* Florence: Vallecchi, 1965. German version: *De Ecclesia: Beiträge zur Konstitution über die Kirche des II. Vatikanischen Konzils.* Freiburg: Herder, 1966.)

Berkouwer, Gerrit C. *The Second Vatican Council and the New Catholicism.* Grand Rapids: W. B. Eerdmans, 1965.

Butler, Christopher. *The Theology of Vatican II.* Revised edition. Westminster, Md.: Christian Classics, 1981.

Congar, Yves M.-J. *Le concile de Vatican II — son Église: Peuple de Dieu et Corps du Christ.* Paris: Beauchesne, 1984.

Dejaifve, Georges. *Un tournant décisif de l'ecclésiologie à Vatican II.* Paris: Beauchesne, 1978.

Dulles, Avery. *The Dimensions of the Church.* Westminster, Md.: Newman, 1967.

Fagin, Gerald M., ed. *Vatican II: Open Questions and New Horizons.* Wilmington, Del.: M. Glazier, 1984. (Articles by A. Dulles, G. Lindbeck, S. Duffy, G. Baum, and F. Cardman.)

Holstein, Henri. *Hiérarchie et Peuple de Dieu d'après "Lumen Gentium".* Paris: Beauchesne, 1970.

Klinger, Elmar, and Wittstadt, Klaus, eds. *Glaube im Pro-zess. Christsein nach dem II. Vatikanum. Für Karl Rahner.* Freiburg: Herder, 1984. (Articles on Vatican II by M.-D. Chenu, Y. M.-J. Congar, G. Alberigo, H. Fries, P. Fransen, and others.)

Kloppenburg, Bonaventure. *The Ecclesiology of Vatican II.* Chicago: Franciscan Herald, 1970.

Lindbeck, George. *The Future of Roman Catholic Theol-olgy.* Philadelphia: Fortress, 1970.

McNamara, Kevin. *Vatican II. The Constitution on the Church: A Theological and Pastoral Commentary.* Chicago: Franciscan Herald, 1968.

Miller, John H., ed. *Vatican II: An Interfaith Appraisal.* Notre Dame, Ind.: University of Notre Dame, 1966. (For matter pertaining to *Lumen Gentium* see the contributions of J. Medina Estevez, H. de Lubac, C. Moeller, G. Philips, Y. M.-J. Congar, C. Colombo, G. Lindbeck, B. Häring, and B. Ahern.)

*Philips, Gérard. *L'Église et son mystère au IIe Concile du Vatican.* 2 vols. Paris: Desclée, 1967.

*Philips, Gérard, Grillmeier, Aloys, Rahner, Karl, Kloster-mann, Ferdinand, Wulf, Friedrich, Semmelroth, Otto, and Ratzinger, Joseph. "Dogmatic Constitu-tion on the Church." In *Commentary on the Docu-ments of Vatican II*, vol. 1, 105-305. Edited by Her-bert Vorgrimler. New York: Herder & Herder, 1967.

Schönmetzer, Adolfus, ed. *Acta congressus internationalis de theologia concilii Vaticani Secundi.* Vatican City:

Typis Polyglottis Vaticanis, 1968. (Articles by H. Schauf, H. de Lubac, K. Rahner, F. A. Sullivan, and others.)

N.B. For the history of the Council consult the well-known works of Xavier Rynne, Henri Fesquet, Antoine Wenger, Michael Novak, Robert B. Kaiser, et al.

17
Twentieth-Century
Roman Catholic Ecclesiology

Adolfs, Robert. *The Grave of God: Has the Church a Future?* London: Burns & Oates, 1967.

Baum, Gregory. *The Credibility of the Church Today.* New York: Herder & Herder, 1968.

Braxton, Edward K. *The Wisdom Community.* New York: Paulist, 1980.

Broucker, José de, ed. *The Suenens Dossier.* Notre Dame, Ind.: Fides, 1970.

Congar, Yves M.-J. "Situation ecclésiologique au moment de 'Ecclesiam suam' et passage à une Église dans l'itinéraire des hommes." In *Ecclesiam suam: Première lettre encyclique de Paul VI*, pp. 79-102. Brescia: Istituto Paolo VI, 1982. (Other articles by R. Aubert, G. Colombo, and others.)

*Dulles, Avery. *A Church to Believe In.* New York: Crossroad, 1982.

_____. *The Resilient Church.* Garden City, N.Y.: Doubleday, 1977.

Frisque, Jean. "L'ecclésiologie au XXe siècle." In *Bilan de la théologie du XXe siècle*, vol. 2, 412-56. Edited by Robert Vander Gucht and Herbert Vorgrimler. Tournai: Casterman, 1970.

Grootaers, Jan. *De Vatican I à Jean Paul II. Le grand tournant de l'Église Catholique.* Paris: Centurion, 1981.

Hebblethwaite, Peter. *The Runaway Church: Post-Conciliar Growth or Decline.* New York: Seabury, 1975.

*Jáki, Stanislas. *Les tendances nouvelles de l'ecclésiologie.* Rome: Herder, 1957.

Küng, Hans. *On Being a Christian.* Garden City, N.Y.: Doubleday, 1976; London: Collins, 1977, 1978. The Church is treated in the following sections: A III, C VII, D I.

Lee, Bernard. *The Becoming of the Church: A Process Theology.* New York: Paulist, 1974.

McBrien, Richard P. *Church: The Continuing Quest.* Paramus, N.J.: Newman, 1970.

_____. *Who Is a Catholic?* Denville, N.J.: Dimension Books, 1967.

MacDonald, Timothy I. *The Ecclesiology of Yves Congar: Foundational Themes.* Lanham, Md.: University Press of America, 1984.

Ménard, Étienne. *L'ecclésiologie: hier et aujourd'hui.* Bruges: Desclée De Brouwer, 1966.

Minnerrath, Roland. *Le droit de l'Église à la liberté du Syllabus à Vatican II.* Paris: Beauchesne, 1982.

O'Dea, Thomas F. *The Catholic Crisis.* Boston: Beacon, 1968.

O'Donovan, Leo J., et al. "A Changing Ecclesiology in a Changing Church: A Symposium on Development in the Ecclesiology of Karl Rahner." *Theological Studies* 38/4 (1977): 736-762. (Articles by J. P. Schineller, J. P. Galvin, and M. A. Fahey.)

Rahner, Karl. *The Christian of the Future.* New York: Herder & Herder, 1967.

_____. *The Church After the Council.* New York: Herder & Herder, 1966.

*_____. *The Shape of the Church to Come.* New York: Seabury, 1974.

_____. *Theological Investigations.* (Especially vols. 2, 5, 6, 10, 12, 14, 17, and 20.) New York: Crossroad; London: Darton, Longman & Todd.

_____. *Theology of Pastoral Action.* New York: Herder & Herder, 1968.

Rikhof, Herwi. *The Concept of the Church.* London: Sheed & Ward; Shepherdstown, W. Va.: Patmos, 1981.

Schillebeeckx, Edward. *God the Future of Man.* New York: Sheed & Ward, 1968; London: Sheed & Ward, 1977.

_____, ed. *L'avenir de l'Église.* Concilium, vol. 60, supplément. Paris: Mame, 1971.

Valeske, Ulrich. *Votum Ecclesiae.* (Part II, pp. 1-210.) Munich: Claudius, 1962.

18
Twentieth-Century
Orthodox Ecclesiology

Ecumenical questions are treated in Section 24.

Afanassieff, Nicolas. *L'Église du Saint Esprit*. Paris: Cerf, 1975.

Benz, Ernst. *The Eastern Orthodox Church*. Garden City, N.Y.: Doubleday Anchor Books, 1963.

Constanteolos, Demetrios. *Understanding the Greek Orthodox Church: Its Faith, History and Practice*. New York: Seabury, 1982.

De Vries, Wilhelm. *Orient et occident: Les structures ecclésiales vues dans l'histoire des sept premiers conciles oecuméniques*. Paris: Cerf, 1974.

Evdokimov, Paul. *L'Orthodoxie*, pp. 123-170. Neuchâtel: Delachaux & Niestlé, 1959.

Fahey, Michael A. "Orthodox Ecumenism and Theology: 1970-78." *Theological Studies* 39 (1978): 446-485.

_____. "Orthodox Ecumenism and Theology: 1978-83." *Theological Studies* 44 (1983): 625-692.

Harakas, Stanley S. "The Local Church: An Eastern Orthodox Perspective." *Ecumenical Review* 29 (1977): 141-153.

Holtzmann, Jerome J. "Eucharistic Ecclesiology of the Orthodox Theologians." *Diakonia* 8 (1973): 5-21.

Lanne, Emmanuel. "Die Kirche als Mysterium und Institution in der Orthodoxen Theologie." In *Mysterium Kirche in der Sicht der theologische Disziplinen*, vol. 2, pp. 891-925. Edited by F. Holböck and T. Sartory. 2 vols. Salzburg: O. Müller, 1962.

Meyendorff, John. *Catholicity and the Church.* Crestwood, N.Y.: St. Vladimir, 1983.

*_____. *The Orthodox Church.* New York: Pantheon Books, 1962.

Nissiotis, Nikos A. "Pneumatological Christology as a Presupposition of Ecclesiology." In *Oecumenica: An Annual Symposium of Ecumenical Research 1967*, pp. 235-252. Minneapolis: Augsburg, 1967.

Patelos, Constantine. *The Orthodox Church in the Ecumenical Movement: Documents and Statements 1902-1975.* Geneva: World Council of Churches, 1978.

*Schmemann, Alexander. *Church, World, Mission: Reflections on Orthodoxy in the West.* Crestwood, N.Y.: St. Vladimir, 1979.

Staniloe, Dumitru. *Theology and the Church.* Crestwood, N.Y.: St. Vladimir, 1984.

Tomos Agapes: Vatican-Phanar (1958-1970). Rome: Polyglotte Vaticane, 1971. (Documentation of the dialogue between the Holy See and the Ecumenical Patriarch of Constantinople.)

Ware, Timothy. *The Orthodox Church*, pp. 243-268. Baltimore, Md.: Penguin, 1963, 1969.

*Zizioulas, J. D. *Being as Communion: Studies in Personhood and the Church.* Crestwood, N.Y.: St. Vladimir, 1980.

_____. "The Pneumatological Dimension of the .Church." *Communio* 1 (1974): 142-158.

19
Twentieth-Century
Protestant and Anglican Ecclesiology

Ecumenical questions are treated in Section 24.

Alston, Wallace M., Jr. *Guides to the Reformed Tradition: The Church*. Atlanta: J. Knox, 1984.

Aulén, Gustav, Fridrichsen, Anton, et al. *Ein Buch von der Kirche*. Göttingen: Vandenhoeck & Ruprecht, 1951. (Swedish scholars on biblical, historical, and systematic aspects of the Church.)

Barth, Karl. *Church Dogmatics*. Vols. IV/1 and IV/2: *The Doctrine of Reconciliation*. Edinburgh: T. & T. Clark, 1956, 1958.

_____. *Theology and Church: Shorter Writings 1920-1928*. London: SCM, 1962.

*Berkouwer, Gerrit C. *The Church*. Grand Rapids: W. B. Eerdmans, 1976.

Bonhoeffer, Dietrich. *The Communion of Saints: A Dogmatic Inquiry into the Sociology of the Church.* New York: Harper & Row, 1963.

Brunner, Emil. *The Misunderstanding of the Church.* London: Lutterworth, 1952.

Ebeling, Gerhard. *Dogmatik des christlichen Glaubens.* vol. 3. Tübingen: J. C. B. Mohr, 1979.

Gilkey, Langdon. *How the Church Can Minister to the World without Losing Itself.* New York: Harper & Row, 1964.

Heinz, Gerhard. *Das Problem der Kirchenentstehung in der deutschen protestantischen Theologie des 20. Jahrhunderts.* Mainz: Matthias-Grünewald, 1974.

Hinson, E. Glenn. *The Integrity of the Church.* Nashville: Broadman, 1978.

Jenkins, Daniel. *The Strangeness of the Church.* Garden City, N.Y.: Doubleday, 1955.

Leith, John H. *The Church: A Believing Fellowship.* Atlanta: J. Knox, 1981.

MacGregor, Geddes. *Corpus Christi: The Nature of the Church according to the Reformed Tradition.* Philadelphia: Westminster, 1958.

*Moltmann, Jürgen. *The Church in the Power of the Spirit.* New York: Harper & Row, 1977. (Cf. *Theological Studies* 34 (1973): 19-35.)

Nelson, J. Robert. *The Realm of Redemption: Studies in the Doctrine of the Nature of the Church in Contemporary Protestant Theology.* London: Epworth, 1951.

Newbigin, Lesslie. *The Household of God.* London: SCM, 1953.

Nygren, Anders. *Christ and His Church.* Philadelphia: Westminster, 1956.

Nygren, Anders, et al. *This Is the Church.* Philadelphia: Muhlenberg, 1962. (Articles by Swedish Lutheran theologians: A. Nygren, G. Aulén, A. Fridrichsen, and others.)

O'Grady, Colm. *The Church in the Theology of Karl Barth.* London: G. Chapman, 1968. (Extensive bibliography.)

_____. *The Church in Catholic Theology: Dialogue with Karl Barth.* London: G. Chapman, 1970.

Pannenberg, Wolfhart. *Thesen zur Theologie der Kirche.* 2nd ed. Munich: Claudius, 1974.

_____. *The Church.* Philadelphia: Westminster, 1983.

Runyon, Theodore, ed. *Hope for the Church: Moltmann in Dialogue with Practical Theology.* Nashville: Abingdon, 1979.

Schlink, Edmund. *The Coming Christ and the Coming Church.* Philadelphia: Fortress, 1968.

Visser't Hooft, Wilhelm A., and Oldham, Joseph. *The Church and Its Function in Society.* Chicago: Willett, Clarke, 1927.

*Welch, Claude. *The Reality of the Church.* New York: Scribner, 1958.

Williams, Colin W. *The Church.* Philadelphia: Westminster, 1958.

20
The Nature of the Church

Only Roman Catholic authors are given here. Orthodox, Protestant, and Anglican works are given in their respective sections.

Antón, Angel. *La Iglesia de Cristo*. Madrid: Biblioteca de autores cristianos, 1977.

Auer, Johann. *Die Kirche — Das allgemeine Heilssakrament*. Regensburg: Pustet, 1983.

Bouyer, Louis. *The Church of God: Body of Christ and Temple of the Holy Spirit*. Chicago: Franciscan Herald, 1982.

Bühlmann, Walbert. *Weltkirche: Neue Dimensionen. Modell für das Jahr 2001*. Graz: Styria, 1984.

Butler, Basil Christopher. *The Idea of the Church*. Baltimore: Helicon, 1962.

Casel, Odo. *Mysterium der Ekklesia*. Mainz: Matthias-Grünewald, 1961.

Congar, Yves, M.-J. *I Believe in the Holy Spirit.* 3 vols. New York: Seabury, 1983; London: G. Chapman, 1983.

_____. *The Mystery of the Church.* Baltimore: Helicon, 1960; 2nd edition, revised 1965.

_____. *The Mystery of the Temple.* Westminster, Md.: Newman, 1967.

_____. *Sainte Église: Etudes et approches ecclésiologiques.* Unam Sanctam, no. 41. Paris: Cerf, 1963. (Articles published over 30 years.)

Dóriga, Enrique L. *Jerarquía, infalibilidad y comunión intereclesial.* Barcelona: Herder, 1973.

*Dulles, Avery. *Models of the Church.* Garden City, N.Y.: Doubleday, 1974; Dublin: Gill & Macmillan, 1976.

Fries, Heinrich. *Aspects of the Church.* Westminster, Md.: Newman, 1966. (A collection of essays on Catholic and ecumenical ecclesiology.)

Journet, Charles. *L'Église du Verbe Incarné.* 3 vols. Bruges: Desclée De Brouwer, 1941, 1951, 1969. (Vol. 1 in English: *The Church of the Incarnate Word.* New York: Sheed & Ward, 1955.)

Kilian, Sabbas. "The Holy Spirit in Christ and in Christians." *American Benedictine Review* 20 (1969): 99-121.

*Küng, Hans. *The Church.* New York: Sheed & Ward, 1968; Tunbridge Wells: Search Press, 1969; (Paperback: Doubleday Image, 1976.) Criticisms and replies in

Diskussion um Hans Küng, 'Die Kirche'. Edited by H. Häring and J. Nolte. Freiburg: Herder, 1971.

Le Guillou, Marie-Joseph. *Christ and Church: A Theology of the Mystery.* New York: Desclée, 1966.

Lubac, Henri de. *Catholicism: A Study of Dogma in Relation to the Corporate Destiny of Mankind.* New York: Longmans, Green, 1950; Tunbridge Wells: Burns & Oates/Wheathampshire: A. Clarke Books.

——————. *The Splendour of the Church.* New York: Sheed & Ward, 1956. Reprinted New York: Paulist Deus Books, 1963; London: Sheed & Ward, 1979.

Maritain, Jacques. *On the Church of Christ: The Person of the Church and Her Personnel.* Notre Dame, Ind.: University of Notre Dame, 1973.

McBrien, Richard. *Do We Need the Church?* New York: Harper & Row, 1969.

——————. *Catholicism,* chapters 17-24. Minneapolis: Winston, 1980; London: G. Chapman, 1980.

McNamara, Kevin. *Sacrament of Salvation.* Chicago: Franciscan Herald Press, 1981.

Mondin, Battista. *Le nuove ecclesiologie.* Rome: Paoline, 1980.

Mühlen, Heribert. *Una Mystica Persona.* 2nd ed. Paderborn: F. Schöningh, 1967. French version: *L'Esprit dans l'Église.* 2 vols. Paris: Cerf, 1969.

Powell, John. *The Mystery of the Church*. Milwaukee: Bruce, 1967.

Proceedings of the Catholic Theological Society of America 39 (1984). (Articles on the World Church by A. Dulles, M. J. Scanlon, L. S. Cahill, W. C. Smith, and G. Wainwright.)

Ruether, Rosemary Radford. *The Church against Itself.* New York: Herder & Herder, 1967.

Salaverri, Ioachim. "De ecclesia Christi." In *Sacrae Theologiae Summa*, 3rd ed., vol. 1, pp. 497-953. Madrid: Biblioteca de autores cristianos, 1955.

Schmaus, Michael. *Katholische Dogmatik.* Vol. III/1. Munich: M. Hueber, 1958.

*_____. *Dogma 4: The Church*. Kansas City: Sheed & Ward, 1972, 1976; London: Sheed & Ward, 1972.

Sullivan, Francis A. *De ecclesia*. Vol. 1: *Questiones theologiae fundamentalis*. Rome: Gregoriana 1963; 2nd edition, 1965.

21
The Church as Body of Christ and People of God

Asmussen, Hans, et al. *Die Kirche Volk Gottes.* Stuttgart: Schwaben, 1961. (Articles by Lutheran and Roman Catholic theologians: H. Asmussen, E. Hesse, W. Lehmann, and others.)

Galot, Jean. *Dans le corps mystique.* Bruges: Desclée De Brouwer, 1961.

Keller, Max. *"Volk Gottes" als Kirchenbegriff. Eine Untersuchung zum neueren Verständnis.* Einsiedeln: Benziger, 1970.

Malmberg, Felix. *Ein Leib — ein Geist.* Freiburg: Herder, 1960.

*Mersch, Emile. *The Theology of the Mystical Body.* St. Louis: B. Herder, 1958.

Mura, Ernest. *The Mystical Body of Christ.* St. Louis: B. Herder, 1963.

Norris, Frank B. *God's Own People: An Introductory Study of the Church*. Baltimore: Helicon, 1962.

Pelton, Robert S., ed. *The Church as the Body of Christ*. Notre Dame, Ind.: University of Notre Dame, 1963. (Articles by W. J. Burghardt, B. Cooke, B. Ahern, K. E. Skydsgaard, and F. H. Littell.)

Ratzinger, Joseph. *Das neue Volk Gottes. Entwürfe zur Ekklesiologie*. Düsseldorf: Patmos, 1969.

Robinson, John A. T. *The Body: A Study in Pauline Theology*. London: SCM, 1952.

*Schillebeeckx, Edward, ed. *The Church and Mankind*. Concilium, no. 1. New York: Paulist, 1965. (Articles by Y. M.-J. Congar, E. Schillebeeckx, R. Schnackenburg.)

Schweizer, Eduard. *The Church as the Body of Christ*. Richmond: J. Knox, 1964.

Tromp, Sebastian. *Corpus Christi quod est ecclesia*. 4 vols. Vol. I: *Introductio generalis* (English translation: New York: Vantage, 1960); Vol. II: *De Christo capite mystici corporis*; Vol. III: *De Spiritu Christi anima*; Vol. IV: *De virgine deipara Maria corde mystici corporis*. Rome: Gregoriana, 1946-1972.

Vidal, Maurice. *L'Église, peuple de Dieu dans l'histoire des hommes*. Paris: Centurion, 1975.

22
The Church as One, Holy, Catholic, and Apostolic

Beinert, Wolfgang. *Um das dritte Kirchenattribut.* 2 vols. Essen: H. Wingen, 1964.

Brière, Yves de la. "Église (Question des Notes)." In *Dictionnaire apologétique de la foi catholique*, vol. 1, col. 1268-1301. Paris: Beauchesne, 1925.

Catholicity and Apostolicity. Special issue of *One in Christ* 6/3 (1970). (Report of the WCC—RC Joint Theological Commission, with articles by R. Schnackenburg, J. Bosc, J. Witte, W. Pannenberg, and others.)

Congar, Yves M.-J. "Catholicité." *Catholicisme*. Vol. 2, pp. 722-725.

_____. L'Église une, sainte, catholique, et apostolique. In *Mysterium Salutis*, no. 15. Paris: Cerf, 1970. German version: "Die Wesenseigenschaften der Kirche." In *Mysterium salutis*, vol. IV/1, 357-599. Edited by Johannes Feiner and Magnus Löhrer. Einsiedeln: Benziger, 1972.

_____. *The Wide World My Parish: Salvation and Its Problems.* Baltimore: Helicon, 1961.

Garciadiego, Alejandro. *Katholiké Ekklesia.* Mexico: Editorial Jus, 1953.

Hastings, Adrian. *One and Apostolic.* New York: Sheed & Ward, 1963.

Küng, Hans, ed. *Apostolic Succession: Rethinking a Barrier to Unity.* Concilium, no. 34. Glen Rock, N.J.: Paulist, 1968.

Lubac, Henri de. *Catholicism: A Study of Dogma in Relation to the Corporate Destiny of Mankind.* New York: Longmans, Green, 1950; Tunbridge Wells: Burns & Oates/Wheathampstead: A. Clarke Books.

Möhler, Johann Adam. *Die Einheit in der Kirche: oder, Das Prinzip des Katholicismus.* New edition. Edited by J. R. Geiselmann. Cologne: Hegner, 1957. (French translation: *L'unité dans l'Église.* Unam Sanctam, no. 2. Paris: Cerf, 1938.)

Neuner, Joseph. "Die Weltkirche: Die Katholizität der Kirche in Missionswerk." In *Mysterium Kirche in der Sicht der theologische Disziplinen,* pp. 815-889. Edited by F. Holböck and T. Sartory. 2 vols. Salzburg: O. Müller, 1962.

Steinacker, Peter. *Die Kennzeichen der Kirche.* Berlin: DeGruyter, 1982.

Thils, Gustave. *Les notes de l'Église dans l'apologétique catholique depuis la Réforme.* Gembloux: J. Duculot, 1937.

Witte, Jan L. "L'Église, Sacramentum Unitatis du cosmos et du genre humain." In *L'Église de Vatican II*, vol. 2, 457-491. Edited by G. Baraúna. 3 vols. Unam Sanctam, no. 51 a, b, and c. Paris: Cerf, 1966. (Italian version: *La Chiesa del Vaticano II*. Florence: Vallecchi, 1965. German version: *De Ecclesia: Beiträge zur Konstitution über die Kirche des II. Vatikanischen Konzils*. Freiburg: Herder, 1966.)

*_____. "One, Holy, Catholic, and Apostolic." In *One, Holy, Catholic, and Apostolic*, pp. 1-43. Edited by Herbert Vorgrimler. London: Sheed and Ward, 1968.

N.B. For holiness and unity of the Church see also Sections 23 and 24 below.

23
The Church as Holy and Sinful

Balthasar, Hans Urs von. "Casta Meretrix." In *Sponsa Verbi: Skizzen zur Theologie*, vol. 2, 203-305. Einsiedeln: Johannes, 1961.

Congar, Yves M.-J. "L'Église est sainte." *Angelicum* 42 (1965): 273-298.

*Latourelle, René. *Christ and the Church: Signs of Salvation*, pp. 211-264. Staten Island, N.Y.: Alba House, 1972.

Laszlo, Stephen. "Sin in the Holy Church of God." In *Council Speeches of Vatican II*, pp. 44-48. Edited by Hans Küng et al. Glen Rock, N.J.: Paulist Deus Books, 1964.

Molinari, Paolo. *Saints: Their Place in the Church*. New York: Sheed & Ward, 1965.

Rahner, Karl. "The Church of the Saints." In *Theological Investigations*, vol. 3, 91-104. New York: Crossroad, 1967; London: Darton, Longman & Todd, 1967.

_____. "The Church of Sinners." In *Theological Investigations*, vol. 6, 253-269. New York: Crossroad, 1969; London: Darton, Longman & Todd, 1969.

*_____. "The Sinful Church in the Decrees of Vatican II." In *Theological Investigations*, vol. 6, 270-294. New York: Crossroad, 1967; London: Darton, Longman & Todd, 1969.

Smith, Robert D. *The Mark of Holiness*. Westminster, Md.: Newman, 1961.

Stöhr, Johannes. "Heilige Kirche — Sündige Kirche?" *Münchener theologische Zeitschrift* 18 (1967): 119-142.

24
The Church as One and Divided

Backman, Milton V., Jr. *Christian Churches of America.
Origins and Beliefs.* New York: C. Scribner's Sons,
1976.

Baum, Gregory. "The Ecclesial Reality of Other Churches."
In *The Church and Ecumenism*, 62-86. Edited by
Hans Küng. Concilium, no. 4. Glen Rock, N.J.: Paulist,
1965.

_____. *Progress and Perspectives.* New York: Sheed
& Ward, 1962. (Paperback: *The Catholic Quest for
Christian Unity.* Glen Rock, N.J.: Paulist Deus
Books, 1965.)

_____. *That They May Be One: A Study of Papal
Doctrine.* Westminster, Md.: Newman, 1958.

*Becker, Werner, and Feiner, Johannes. "Decree on Ecumen-
ism." In *Commentary on the Documents of Vatican
II*, vol. 2, 1-164. Edited by Herbert Vorgrimler. New
York: Herder & Herder, 1968.

Brown, Robert McAfee. *The Ecumenical Revolution.* Revised Edition. Garden City, N.Y.: Doubleday Image Books, 1969; First Edition, Garden City, N.Y.: Doubleday, 1967. Tunbridge Wells: Burns & Oates/Wheathampshire: A. Clarke Books.

Butler, Basil Christopher. *The Church and Unity. An Essay.* London: G. Chapman, 1979.

Congar, Yves M.-J. *Dialogue Between Christians.* Westminster, Md.: Newman, 1966. (A collection of previously published articles with a new introduction.)

_____. *Diversités et communion.* Paris: Cerf, 1982. (English translation in production.)

*_____. *Divided Christendom: A Catholic Study of the Problem of Reunion.* London: G. Bles, 1939.

Dulles, Avery. "The Church, the Churches, and the Catholic Church." *Theological Studies* 33 (1972): 199-234.

Flew, Robert Newton, ed. *The Nature of the Church.* Papers presented to the Third World Conference on Faith and Order. New York: Harper, 1952.

Fries, Heinrich. "Church and Churches." In *Problems and Perspectives of Fundamental Theology,* pp. 309-326. Edited by René Latourelle and Gerald O'Collins. New York: Paulist, 1982.

Fries, Heinrich, and Rahner, Karl. *Einigung der Kirchen — reale Möglichkeit.* Freiburg: Herder, 1983. (English translation in production.)

Le Guillou, Marie-Joseph. *Mission et unité: exigences de la communion.* Unam Sanctam, nos. 33-34. Paris: Cerf, 1960.

McDonnell, Kilian. "The Concept of 'Church' in the Documents of Vatican II as Applied to Protestant Denominations." *Worship* 44 (1970): 332-349. Also found in Paul C. Empie and T. Austin Murphy, eds. *Eucharist and Ministry: Lutherans and Catholics in Dialogue* IV, pp. 307-324. Minneapolis: Augsburg, 1979.

McGovern, James O. *The Church in the Churches.* Washington, D.C.: Corpus, 1968.

Mühlen, Heribert. "Der eine Geist Christi und die vielen Kirchen." In *Una Mystica Persona*, pp. 494-567. 2nd ed. Paderborn: F. Schöningh, 1967. French version: "L'unique Esprit du Christ et les multiples Églises." In *L'Esprit dans l'Église*, vol. 2, 175-263. Paris: Cerf, 1969.

_____. *Morgen wird Einheit sein.* Paderborn: F. Schöningh, 1967.

Minus, Paul. *The Catholic Rediscovery of Protestantism. A History of Roman Catholic Ecumenical Pioneering.* New York: Paulist, 1976.

*Thils, Gustave. *L'Église et les Églises: perspectives nouvelles.* Bruges: Desclée De Brouwer, 1967.

Thurian, Max, ed. *Ecumenical Perspectives on Baptism, Eucharist and Ministry.* Geneva: World Council of Churches, 1983. (Articles by L. Vischer, E. Lanne, G. Wainwright, A. Houtepen, and others.)

Wainwright, Geoffrey. *The Ecumenical Moment: Crisis and Opportunity for the Church.* Grand Rapids: W. B. Eerdmans, 1983.

World Council of Churches. *Man's Disorder and God's Design.* Vol. 1: *The Universal Church in God's Design.* Papers prepared for the First Assembly of the World Council of Churches, Amsterdam, Holland. New York: Herder, 1949.

World Council of Churches. *Baptism, Eucharist and Ministry.* Faith and Order Paper, no. 111. Geneva: World Council of Churches, 1982.

World Council of Churches. *Handbook of Member Churches.* Geneva: World Council of Churches, 1982.

N.B. Studies of the Ecumenical Movement are too numerous to be listed here.

25
Membership in the Church

Carrier, Hervé. *The Sociology of Religious Belonging*. New York: Herder & Herder, 1965.

Dejaifve, Georges. "L'appartenance à l'Église du Concile de Florence à Vatican II." *Nouvelle revue théologique* 99 (1977): 21-50.

*Dulles, Avery. *Church Membership as a Catholic and Ecumenical Problem*. Milwaukee: Marquette University, 1981.

_____. *The Resilient Church*. Chapter 7, pp. 133-151; Appendix II, pp. 196-198. Garden City, N.Y.: Doubleday, 1977; Dublin: Gill & Macmillan, 1978.

Internationale katholische Zeitschrift Communio, 5/3 (1976). Theme issue on Church membership with articles by K. Lehmann, Y. M.-J. Congar, J. Ratzinger, and H. U. von Balthasar.

Menges, Walter, and Greinacher, Norbert. *Die Zugehörigkeit zur Kirche*. Mainz: Matthias-Grünewald, 1964.

O'Neill, Colman E. "St. Thomas on the Membership of the Church." *Thomist* 27 (1963): 88-140.

Rahner, Karl. "Kirchengliedschaft. II. Dogmatisch." In *Lexikon für Theologie und Kirche*, vol. 6, col. 223-225. Freiburg: Herder, 1961.

_____. "Membership of the Church According to the Teaching of Pius XII's Encyclical, 'Mystici Corporis Christi.'" In *Theological Investigations*, vol. 2, 1-88. New York: Crossroad, 1963; London: Darton, Longman & Todd, 1963.

Sauras, Emilio. "Church. 5. Membership of the Church." In *Sacramentum Mundi*, vol. 1, 332-337. New York: Herder & Herder, 1968. (Bibliography.)

_____. "The Members of the Church." *The Thomist* 27 (1963): 78-87.

Willems, Boniface. "Who Belongs to the Church?" In *The Church and Mankind*, 131-151. Edited by Edward Schillebeeckx. Concilium, no. 1. Glen Rock, N.J.: Paulist, 1965. (Survey of literature.)

26
The Church and Salvation:
Necessity of the Church

*Burghardt, Walter J., and Thompson, William G., eds. *Why the Church?* New York: Paulist, 1977. (Reprint from *Theological Studies* 37/4 (1976).) (Articles by J. P. Schineller, E. A. LaVerdiere and W. G. Thompson; J. P. Burns; R. D. Haight, and R. T. Sears.)

Congar, Yves M.-J. "No Salvation Outside the Church?" In *The Wide World My Parish: Salvation and Its Problems*. Baltimore: Helicon, 1961.

Eminyan, Maurice. *The Theology of Salvation*. Boston: Daughters of St. Paul, 1960.

Fenton, Joseph C. *The Catholic Church and Salvation in the Light of Recent Pronouncements by the Holy See*. Westminster, Md.: Newman, 1958.

Kern, Walter. *Ausserhalb der Kirche kein Heil?* Freiburg: Herder, 1979.

King, John J. *The Necessity of the Church for Salvation in Selected Writings of the Past Century.* Washington, D.C.: Catholic University of America, 1960.

Lombardi, Riccardo. *The Salvation of the Unbeliever.* Westminster, Md.: Newman, 1960.

Rahner, Karl. For articles on the salvation of non-Christians and Anonymous Christianity see *Theological Investigations*, vols. 1, 5, 6, 12, 14, and 16. New York: Crossroad; London: Darton, Longman & Todd.

Röper, Anita. *The Anonymous Christian.* New York: Sheed & Ward, 1966.

Schlette, Heinz Robert. *Towards a Theology of Religions.* New York: Herder & Herder, 1966.

*Theisen, Jerome P. *The Ultimate Church and the Promise of Salvation.* Collegeville, Minn.: St. John's University, 1976.

27
The Church and Missionary Activity

Anderson, Gerald H., *Bibliography of the Theology of Missions in the Twentieth Century.* Third edition, revised and enlarged. New York: Missionary Research Library, 1966.

_____. ed. *The Theology of Christian Mission.* New York: McGraw-Hill, 1961; paperback edition, 1965.

Anderson, Gerald H., and Stransky, Thomas F., eds. *Mission Trends.* Nos. 1ff. New York: Paulist, 1974ff.

Blauw, Johannes. *The Missionary Nature of the Church.* New York/London: McGraw-Hill, 1962.

Bohr, David. *Evangelization in America.* New York: Paulist, 1977.

Braaten, Carl E. *The Flaming Center: A Theology of Christian Mission.* Philadelphia: Fortress, 1977.

Brechter, Suso. "Decree on the Church's Missionary Activity." In *Commentary on the Documents of Vatican II*, vol. 4, 87-181. Edited by Herbert Vorgrimler. New York: Herder & Herder, 1969.

*Bühlmann, Walbert. *The Coming of the Third Church*. Maryknoll, N.Y.: Orbis, 1977.

——————. *Courage Church*. Maryknoll, N.Y.: Orbis, 1978.

——————. *God's Chosen Peoples*. Maryknoll, N.Y.: Orbis, 1982; Middlegreen: St. Paul, 1982.

——————. *The Missions on Trial*. Maryknoll, N.Y.: Orbis, 1979.

Comblin, Joseph. *The Meaning of Mission: Jesus, Christians, and the Wayfaring Church*. Maryknoll, N.Y.: Orbis, 1977; Dublin: Gill & Macmillan, 1979.

Costas, Orlando E. *The Integrity of Mission: The Inner Life and Outreach of the Church*. San Francisco: Harper & Row, 1979.

Cotter, James P., ed. *The Word in the Third World*. Washington, D.C.: Corpus, 1968.

Davies, John G. *Worship and Mission*. New York: Association Press, 1967.

Dhavamony, Mariasusai, ed. *Prospettive di missiologia oggi*. Rome: Gregoriana, 1982.

Donovan, Vincent J. *Christianity Rediscovered*. Maryknoll, N.Y.: Orbis, 1978; London: SCM, 1982.

Fahey, Michael A., "The Mission of the Church: To Divinize or To Humanize?" *Proceedings of the Catholic Theological Society of America* 31 (1967): 56-69.

*Flanagan, Padraig, ed. *A New Missionary Era*. Maryknoll, N.Y.: Orbis, 1982. (Articles by E. McDonagh, J. Comblin, B. Hearne, W. Bühlmann, and others.)

Glasser, Arthur F., and McGavran, Donald A. *Contemporary Theologies of Mission*. Grand Rapids: Baker, 1983.

Greinacher, Norbert, and Müller, Alois, eds. *Evangelization in the World Today*. Concilium, No. 114. New York: Seabury, 1979.

Hahn, Ferdinand. *Mission in the New Testament*. Studies in Biblical Literature, no. 47. Naperville, Ill.: Allenson, 1958; London: SCM, 1981.

Hale, J. Russell. *The Unchurched: Who They Are and Why They Stay Away*. New York: Harper & Row, 1980.

Hastings, Adrian. *Church and Mission in Modern Africa*. London: Burns & Oates, 1967; New York: Fordham University Press, 1980.

Hillman, Eugene. *The Church as Mission*. New York: Herder & Herder, 1965.

_____. *The Wider Ecumenism*. London: Burns & Oates, 1968.

Hocking, William E., ed. *Re-Thinking Missions: A Layman's Inquiry after 100 Years*. New York: Harper, 1932.

Hoekendijk, Johannes C. *The Church Inside Out.* Philadelphia: Westminster, 1966.

Hoffman, Ronan. *Pioneer Theories of Mission.* Washington, D.C.: Catholic University of America, 1960.

Illich, Ivan. *The Church, Change, and Development.* Chicago: Urban Training Center, 1970.

The Jurist, 39/1-2 (1979). Entire issue devoted to "The Church as Mission." (Articles by J. H. Provost, R. D. Haight, D. Bohr, C. F. Jegen, J. A. Coleman, and others.)

Luzbetak, Louis. *The Church and Cultures. An Applied Anthropology for the Religious Worker.* Techny, Ill.: Divine Word, 1963.

McDonagh, Enda, ed. *The Church is Mission.* Cleveland: World, 1969.

Motte, Mary, and Lang, Joseph R., eds. *Mission in Dialogue.* The SEDOS Research Seminar on the Future of Mission. Maryknoll, N.Y.: Orbis, 1982.

*Paul VI. Apostolic Exhortation *On Evangelization in the Modern World.* Washington, D.C.: USCC, 1976.

*Power, John. *Mission Theology Today.* Maryknoll: Orbis, 1971.

Rahner, Karl. "Grundprinzipien zur heutigen Mission der Kirche." In *Handbuch der Pastoraltheologie.* vol. 2, 46-80. Edited by F. X. Arnold, et al. Freiburg: Herder, 1966.

_____, ed. *Rethinking the Church's Mission.* Concilium, no. 13. Glen Rock, N.J.: Paulist, 1966.

Roozen, David A. *The Churched and the Unchurched in America.* Washington, D.C.: Glenmary Research Center, 1978.

Senior, Donald, and Stuhlmueller, Carroll. *The Biblical Foundations for Mission.* Maryknoll, N.Y.: Orbis, 1983; London: SCM Press, 1983.

Seumois, André. *Théologie missionaire.* 5 vols. Rome: Urbaniana, 1973-81.

Shorter, Aylward. *The Theology of Mission.* Notre Dame, Ind.: Fides, 1972; Cork: Mercier Press, 1973.

Sweazey, George E. *The Church as Evangelist.* San Fransisco/London: Harper & Row, 1984.

N.B. See also below Sections 49 and 50.

28
The Church and Sacramentality

Boff, Leonardo. *Die Kirche als Sakrament im Horizont der Welterfahrung.* Paderborn: F. Schöningh, 1972.

Congar, Yves M.-J. "L'ecclesia' ou communauté chrétienne, sujet intégral de l'action liturgique." In *La liturgie après Vatican II,* 241-282. Edited by Yves Congar and Jean Pierre Jossua. Unam Sanctam, no. 66. Paris: Cerf, 1967.

_____. *Un peuple messianique: L'Église sacrament du salut, salut et liberation.* Paris: Cerf, 1975.

Dulles, Avery. "The Church: Sacrament and Ground of Faith." In *Problems and Perspectives of Fundamental Theology,* pp. 259-273. Edited by René Latourelle and Gerald O'Collins. New York: Paulist, 1982.

Elert, Werner. *Eucharist and Church Fellowship in the First Four Centuries.* St. Louis: Concordia, 1966.

Forte, B. *La chiesa nell'Eucharistia. Per un'ecclesiologia eucharistica alla luce del Vaticano II.* Naples: D'Auria, 1975.

Häring, Bernard. *Sacraments and Your Everyday Life.* Liguori, Mo.: Liguori, 1976.

Kasper, Walter. "Die Kirche als universales Sakrament des Heils." In *Glaube im Prozess: Christsein nach dem 11. Vatikanum. Für Karl Rahner.* pp. 221-239. Edited by Elmar Klinger and Klaus Wittstadt. Freiburg: Herder, 1984.

*Latourelle, René. *Christ and the Church: Signs of Salvation.* Staten Island, N.Y.: Alba House, 1972.

Lubac, Henri de. *Corpus Mysticum: L'eucharistie et l'Église au moyen âge.* Paris: Aubier, 1944.

Navarro Lisbona, Antonio. *La Iglesia sacramento de Cristo sacerdote.* Salamanca: Sigueme, 1965.

Przewozny, Bernard. *Church as the Sacrament of the Unity of All Mankind in "Lumen Gentium" and "Gaudium et Spes" and in Semmelroth, Schillebeeckx, and Rahner.* Rome: Miscellanea Francescana, 1979.

*Rahner, Karl. *The Church and the Sacraments.* New York: Crossroad, 1963; Tunbridge Wells: Burns & Oates, 1974.

*Schillebeeckx, Edward. *Christ the Sacrament of the Encounter with God.* New York: Sheed & Ward, 1963.

Semmelroth, Otto. *Church and Sacrament.* Notre Dame, Ind.: Fides, 1965.

_____. *Die Kirche als Ursakrament.* Frankfurt: J. Knecht, 1953. (French translation: *L'Église sacrement de la rédemption.* Paris: S. Paul, 1963.)

Smulders, Peter. "L'Église sacrement du salut." In *L'Église de Vatican II*, vol. 2, 313-338. Edited by G. Baraúna. 3 vols. Unam Sanctam, no. 51 a, b, and c. Paris: Cerf, 1966. (Italian version: *La Chiesa del Vaticano II*. Florence: Vallecchi, 1965. German version: *De Ecclesia: Beiträge zur Konstitution über die Kirche des II. Vatikanischen Konzils*. Freiburg: Herder, 1966.)

Vollert, Cyril. "The Church and the Sacraments." *Proceedings of the Society of Catholic Teachers of Sacred Doctrine* 8 (1962): 38-58.

29
The Church as Communion

Acerbi, Antonio. *Due ecclesiologie. Ecclesiologia giuridica ed ecclesiologia di communione nella "Lumen gentium".* Bologna: Dehoniane, 1975.

Hamer, Jerôme. *The Church is a Communion.* New York: Sheed & Ward, 1964.

Hertling, Ludwig. *Communio: Church and Papacy in Early Christianity.* Introduction by Jared Wicks. Chicago: Loyola University, 1972.

The Jurist 1-2 (1976). Entire issue is on "The Church as Communion." (Articles by J. H. Provost, M. A. Fahey, T. G. Bissonnette, and others.)

Klostermann, Ferdinand. *Gemeinde — Kirche der Zukunft. Thesen, Dienste, Modelle.* 2 vols. Freiburg: Herder, 1975.

30
Basic Communities

The authors in this section apply the idea of communion given above.

Barbé, Dominique. *Demain, les communautés de base.* Paris: Cerf, 1970.

Barreiro, Alvaro. *Basic Ecclesial Communities: The Evangelization of the Poor.* Maryknoll, N.Y.: Orbis, 1982.

Bissonnette, Tomas G. "Comunidades Eclesiales de Base: Some Contemporary Attempts to Build Ecclesial Koinonia." *Jurist* 36 1/2 (1976): 24-58.

Boff, Clodovis. "The Nature of Basic Christian Communities." In *Tensions between the Church of the First World and the Third World*, 53-58. Edited by Virgilio Elizondo and Norbert Greinacher. Concilium, no. 144. New York: Seabury, 1981.

Boff, Leonardo. *Eclesiogenêse. As comunidades eclesiales de base reinventam a Igreja.* Petrópolis, RJ, Brazil: Vozes, 1977. (French version: *Église en genèse: Les communautés de base réinventent l'Église.* Paris: Desclée, 1978.) An English translation of most of this book — all the material on basic communities — is published as: "Ecclesiogenesis: Ecclesial Basic Communities Re-Invent the Church." *Mid-Stream* 20 (1981): 431-488.

Clark, Stephen B. *Building Christian Communities.* Notre Dame, Ind.: Ave Maria, 1972.

Costello, Gerald M. *Mission to Latin America.* Maryknoll, N.Y.: Orbis, 1979.

Delespesse, Max. *The Church Community: Leaven and Life Style.* Ottawa: Catholic Centre of St. Paul University, 1969.

Latin American Documentation. *Basic Christian Communities.* Ladoc "Keyhole" Series. Washington, D.C.: USCC, 1976; Liverpool: Liverpool Institute of Socio-Religious Studies, 1978.

Marins, José, and Trevisan, T. M. *Comunidades Eclesiales de Base.* Bogotá: Paulinas, 1975.

Metz, Johann Baptist. *The Emergent Church*, pp. 82-94. New York: Crossroad: 1981; London: SCM, 1981.

National Federation of Priests' Councils. *Developing Basic Christian Communities: A Handbook.* Chicago: NFPC, 1979.

National Secretariat for Hispanic Affairs (USCC/NCCB). *Comunidades Eclesiales de Base en los Estados Unidos (Basic Ecclesial Communities: An Experience in the United States).* Liguori, Mo.: 1980.

Perrin-Jassey, Marie-France. *Basic Community in the African Churches.* Maryknoll, N.Y.: Orbis, 1973.

*Pro Mundi Vita 50(1974): Basic Christian Communities in the Church.

*Torres, Sergio, and Eagleson, John, eds. *The Challenge of Basic Christian Communities.* Maryknoll, N.Y.: Orbis, 1981.

Vela, Jesús Andrés. *Comunidades de base, Conversión a qué?* Second Edition. Bogotá: Ediciones Paulinas, 1973.

31
The Church as Institution and Structure

References to a sociological analysis of the Church are given below in Section 33.

*Baum, Gregory, and Greeley, Andrew, eds. *The Church as Institution.* Concilium, no. 91. New York: Herder & Herder, 1974.

Congar, Yves M.-J. *Droit ancien et structures ecclésiales.* London: Variorum Reprints, 1982. (Contains several articles by Congar.)

Defois, Gérard. *Le pouvoir dans l'Église: Analyse institutionnelle, historique et théologique.* Paris: Cerf, 1973.

Dombois, Hans. *Hierarchie. Grund und Grenze einer Umstrittenen Struktur.* Freiburg: Herder, 1971.

Dulles, Avery. "Institution and Charism in the Church." In *A Church to Believe In*, chapter 2. New York: Crossroad, 1982.

L'Église: Institution et foi. Brussels: Publications des Facultés universitaires Saint-Louis, 1979.

*Granfield, Patrick. "The Church as Institution: A Reformulated Model." *Journal of Ecumenical Studies* 16 (1978): 425-447.

_____. "The Church as Societas Perfecta in the Schemata of Vatican I." *Church History* 46 (1979): 431-446.

_____. "The Rise and Fall of Soçietas Perfecta." In *May Church Ministers be Politicians?*, 3-8. Edited by Peter Huizing and Knut Walf. Concilium, no. 157. New York: Seabury, 1982.

Jiménez-Urresti, Teodoro, ed. *Structures of the Church.* Concilium, no. 58. New York: Herder & Herder, 1970.

Kaufmann, Franz-Xaver. *Kirche Begreifen. Analysen und Thesen zur gesellschaftlichen Verfassung des Christentums.* Freiburg: Herder, 1979.

Kehl, Medard. *Kirche als Institution: Zur theologischen Begrundüng des institutionellen Charakters der Kirche in der neueren deutschsprachigen katholischen Ekklesiologie.* Frankfurt: J. Knecht, 1976.

*Küng, Hans. *Structures of the Church.* New York: T. Nelson, 1964; Paperback: University of Notre Dame, 1968.

Navarrette, Urban. "Potestas vicaria ecclesiae. Evolutio historica conceptus atque observationes attenta doctrina concilii Vaticani II." *Periodica de re morali, canonica, liturgica* 60 (1971): 415-486.

Pouvoirs. Revue française d'études constitutionnelles et politiques 17 (1981). (Entire issue devoted to "Le pouvoir dans l'Église." Articles by G. Defois, E. Poulat, J. Gausemet, J.-L. Harouel, and others.)

Schwartz, Reinhold. "De potestate propria ecclesiae." *Periodica de re morali, canonica, liturgica* 63 (1974): 429-455.

Walf, Knut. "Die katholische Kirche — eine 'societas perfecta'." *Theologische Quartalschrift* 157 (1977): 107-118.

Zimmerman, Marie. "Stabilisation d'un modèle de société. La 'société parfaite'." In *Structure sociale et Église*, pp. 25-48. Strasbourg: Cerdic, 1981.

32
Continuity, Structural Change, and Reform

Chirico, Peter. "Priesthood, Eucharist, Hierarchy: Instantaneous or Emerging?" *Chicago Studies* 16 (1977): 265-277.

*Congar, Yves M.-J. *Vraie et fausse Réforme dans l'Église.* Unam Sanctam, no. 20. Paris: Cerf, 1950.

Dulles, Avery. "*Ius divinum* as an Ecumenical Problem." *Theological Studies* 38 (1977): 681-708. Reprinted in *A Church to Believe In*, chapter 6. New York: Crossroad, 1982.

_____. *The Resilient Church*, chapter 2, pp. 29-44. Garden City, N.Y.: Doubleday, 1977; Dublin: Gill & Macmillan, 1978.

*Fahey, Michael A. "Continuity in the Church amid Structural Changes." *Theological Studies* 35 (1974): 415-440.

Greinacher, Norbert, and Müller, Alois, eds. *Ongoing Reform in the Church*, Concilium, no. 73. New York: Herder & Herder, 1972.

Küng, Hans. *The Council, Reform, and Reunion.* New York: Sheed & Ward, 1962.

McBrien, Richard P. *The Remaking of the Church.* New York: Harper & Row, 1973.

O'Malley, John W. "Reform, Historical Consciousness, and Vatican II's *Aggiornamento*." *Theological Studies* 32 (1971): 573-601.

_____. "Developments, Reforms, and Two Great Reformations: Towards a Historical Assessment of Vatican II." *Theological Studies* 44 (1983): 373-406.

Peter, Carl J. "Dimensions of *Jus Divinum* in Roman Catholic Theology." *Theological Studies* 34 (1973): 227-250.

*Rahner, Karl. "Basic Observations on the Subject of Changeable and Unchangeable Factors in the Church." In *Theological Investigations*, vol. 14, 3-23. New York: Crossroad, 1976; London: Darton, Longman & Todd, 1976.

_____. "Reflections on the Concept of 'Jus Divinum' in Catholic Thought." In *Theological Investigations*, vol. 5, 219-243. New York: Crossroad, 1966; London: Darton, Longman & Todd, 1966.

33
Sociology of Church

The following titles are in addition to items listed under New Testament (8), Membership in the Church (25), and the Church as Institution and Structure (31).

Baum, Gregory. "The Impact of Sociology on Catholic Theology." *Proceedings of the Catholic Theological Society of America* 30 (1975): 1-29. Responses by Patrick J. Burns and Mary I. Buckley, 31-47.

Berger, Peter L. *The Noise of Solemn Assemblies.* Garden City, N.Y.: Doubleday, 1961.

_____. *A Rumor of Angels.* Garden City, N.Y.: Doubleday, 1970.

*_____. *The Sacred Canopy: Elements of a Sociological Theory of Religion.* Garden City, N.Y.: Doubleday, 1967.

Burns, Patrick J. "Precarious Reality: Ecclesiological Reflections on Peter Berger." *Theology Digest* 21 (1973): 322-333.

Coleman, John A. *An American Strategic Theology.* New York: Paulist, 1982.

Fichter, Joseph. *Organization Man in the Church.* Cambridge: Schenkman, 1974.

_____. *Southern Parish.* Chicago: University of Chicago, 1951.

Greeley, Andrew M. *The American Catholic: A Social Portrait.* New York: Basic Books, 1977.

_____. *The Communal Catholic: A Personal Manifesto.* New York: Seabury, 1976.

_____. *The Denominational Society: A Sociological Approach to Religion in America.* Glenview, Ill.: Scott, Foresman, 1972.

*Gustafson, James M. *Treasure in Earthen Vessels: The Church as a Human Community.* New York: Harper & Row, 1961.

Houtart, François, and Rémy, Jean. *Église et société en mutation.* Paris: Mame, 1969.

Kee, Howard Clark. *Christian Origins in Sociological Perspective.* Philadelphia: Westminster, 1980.

*Komonchak, Joseph A. "Ecclesiology and Social Theory: A Methodological Essay." *The Thomist* 45 (1981): 262-283.

Martin, David A. *The Breaking of the Image: A Sociology of Christian Theory and Practice.* New York: St. Martin, 1980; Oxford: Blackwell, 1982.

7/403

Moberg, David O. *The Church as Social Institution: The Sociology of American Religion.* Englewood Cliffs, N.J.: Prentice-Hall, 1962.

Niebuhr, H. Richard. *The Social Sources of Denominationalism.* New York: H. Holt, 1927. Reprint New York: Meridian Books, 1957; New American Library, 1980.

O'Dea, Thomas F. *Sociology and the Study of Religion.* New York: Basic Books, 1970.

Richey, Russell E., ed. *Denominationalism.* Nashville: Abingdon, 1977.

Troeltsch, Ernst. *The Social Teaching of the Christian Churches.* 2 vols. New York: Macmillan, 1930. Reprint Chicago: University of Chicago, 1981.

Varacalli, Joseph A. *Toward the Establishment of Liberal Catholicism in America.* Washington, D.C.: University Press of America, 1983.

Weber, Max. *From Max Weber.* Edited by H. H. Gerth and C. W. Mills. New York: Oxford University, 1946; London: Routledge & Kegan Paul, 1948, 1970.

Wilson, Bryan R. *Religion in Sociological Perspective.* New York:/Oxford: Oxford University, 1982.

Winter, Gibson. *The Suburban Captivity of the Churches.* New York: Doubleday, 1961.

Zimmermann, Marie. *Structure et Église.* Starsbourg: Cerdic, 1981.

34
Freedom and Participation in the Church

Bassett, William, and Huizing, Peter, eds. *Judgment in the Church*. Concilium, no. 107. New York: Herder & Herder, 1977.

Corecco, Eugenio, et al. *Les droits fondamentaux du chrétien dans l'Église et dans la société*. Fribourg: Éditions universitaires, 1982.

*Coriden, James A., ed. *We the People of God. A Study of Constitutional Government in the Church*. Huntington, Ind.: Canon Law Society of America, 1968.

Curran, Charles E., and Hunt, Robert E. *Dissent in and for the Church*. New York: Sheed & Ward, 1970.

Drane, James F. *Authority and Institution: A Study in Church Crisis*. Milwaukee: Bruce, 1969.

*Granfield, Patrick. *Ecclesial Cybernetics: A Study of Democracy in the Church*. New York: Macmillan, 1973.

Küng, Hans. *Freedom Today.* New York: Sheed & Ward, 1966.

Moltmann, Jürgen, and Küng, Hans, eds. *Who Has the Say in the Church?* Concilium, no. 148. New York: Seabury, 1981.

Müller, Alois, ed. *Democratization of the Church.* Concilium, no. 63. New York: Herder & Herder, 1971.

Orna, Mary Virginia. *Cybernetics, Society, and the Church.* Dayton: Pflaum, 1969.

Rahner, Karl. *Free Speech in the Church.* New York: Sheed & Ward, 1960; London: Greenwood Press, 1981.

Swidler, Leonard. *Freedom in the Church.* Dayton: Pflaum, 1969.

35
The Papacy

Anglican-Roman Catholic International Commission. *The Final Report*. Washington, D.C.: USCC, 1982; London: Catholic Truth Society, 1982; London: SPCK, 1982.

Alberigo, Giuseppe, ed. *Renouveau ecclésial et service papal à la fin du XXe siècle*. Concilium, no. 108 (French edition). Paris: Beauchesne, 1975.

Allmen, Jean Jacques von. *La primauté de Pierre et Paul. Remarques d'un protestant*. Fribourg, Suisse: Editions universitaires, 1977.

Arbeitsgemeinschaft ökumenischer Universitätsinstitute. *Papsttum als ökumenische Frage*. Munich: Kaiser, 1979; Mainz: Matthias-Grünewald, 1979.

Batiffol, Pierre. *Cathedra Petri: études d'histoire ancienne de l'Église*. Unam Sanctam, no. 4. Paris: Cerf, 1938.

Brandenburg, Albert, and Urban, Hans Jörg, eds. *Petrus und Papst*. Münster: Aschendorff, 1977.

Brown, Raymond E., Donfried, Karl P., and Reumann, John, eds. *Peter in the New Testament.* Minneapolis: Augsburg, New York: Paulist, 1973; London: G. Chapman, 1974.

Burn-Murdoch, Hector. *The Development of the Papacy.* New York: Praeger, 1954.

Denzler, Georg, ed. *Das Papsttum in der Diskussion.* Regensburg: Pustet, 1974.

de Satgé, John. *Peter and the Single Church.* London: SPCK, 1981.

Empie, Paul C., and Murphy, T. Austin, eds. *Papal Primacy and the Universal Church.* Lutherans and Catholics in Dialogue, vol. 5. Minneapolis: Augsburg, 1974.

Ernst, Cornelius. "The Primacy of Peter: Theology and Ideology." *New Blackfriars* 50 (1969): 347-355; 399-404.

Franzen, August, and Bäumer, Remigius. *Papstgeschichte. Das Petrusamt in seiner Idee und seiner geschichtlichen Verwirklichung in der Kirche.* Freiburg: Herder, 1974.

*Granfield, Patrick. *The Papacy in Transition.* Garden City, N.Y.: Doubleday, 1980; Dublin: Gill & Macmillan, 1981. (Extensive bibliography.)

Hardt, Michael. *Papsttum und Ökumene. Ansätze eines Neuverständnisses für einen Papstprimat in der protestantischen Theologie des 20. Jahrhunderts.* Paderborn: F. Schöningh, 1981.

Jalland, Trevor Gervase. *The Church and the Papacy.* London: SPCK, 1944.

Küng, Hans, ed. *Papal Ministry in the Church.* Concilium, no. 64. New York: Herder & Herder, 1971.

Maccarrone, Michele. *Vicarius Christi: Storia del titolo papale.* Rome: Facultas theologica pontificii athenaei lateranensis, 1952.

Markus, Robert, and John, Eric. *Pastors or Princes: A New Look at the Papacy and Hierarchy.* Washington, D.C.: Corpus, 1968.

*McCord, Peter J., ed. *A Pope for All Christians?* New York: Paulist, 1976. (Articles by A. Dulles, J. Burgess, J. Meyendorff, J. R. Nelson, and others.)

Meyendorff, John, et al. *The Primacy of Peter in the Orthodox Church.* Leighton Buzzard, Eng.: Faith, 1963; 1973.

Miller, J. Michael. *The Divine Right of the Papacy in Recent Ecumenical Theology.* Rome: Gregoriana, 1980.

_____. *What Are They Saying about Papal Primacy?* New York: Paulist, 1983.

Mund, Hans-Joachim, ed. *Das Petrusamt in der gegenwärtigen Diskussion.* Paderborn: F. Schöningh, 1976.

Mussner, Franz. *Petrus und Paulus — Pole der Einheit.* Freiburg: Herder, 1976.

Ohlig, Karl-Heinz. *Why We Need the Pope.* St. Meinrad: Abbey, 1975.

Pennington, Kenneth. *Pope and Bishops: The Papal Monarchy in the Twelfth and Thirteenth Centuries.* Philadelphia: University of Pennsylvania, 1984.

Pottmeyer, Hermann-Josef. *Unfehlbarkeit und Souveränität: Die päpstliche Unfehlbarkeit im System der ultramontanen Ekklesiologie des 19. Jahrhunderts.* Mainz: Matthias-Grünewald, 1975.

Sherrard, Philip. *Church, Papacy, and Schism: A Theological Inquiry.* London: SPCK, 1978.

Thils, Gustave. *La primauté pontificale.* Gembloux: J. Duculot, 1972.

*Tillard, Jean M. R. *The Bishop of Rome.* Wilmington, Del.: M. Glazier, 1983; London: SPCK, 1983.

Ullmann, Walter. *The Growth of Papal Government in the Middle Ages.* London: Methuen, 1955.

_____. *A Short History of the Papacy in the Middle Ages.* London: Methuen, 1972.

36
Episcopacy and Collegiality

Anciaux, Paul. *The Episcopate in the Church*. Dublin: Gill & Sons, 1965.

Bertrams, Wilhelm. *The Papacy, the Episcopacy, and Collegiality*. Westminster, Md.: Newman, 1964.

Betti, Umberto. *La dottrina sull'episcopato del capitolo III della costitutione dommatica Lumen Gentium*. Rome: Città nuova, 1968.

Bouëssé, Humbert, and Mandouze, André, eds. *L'évêque dans l'Église du Christ*. Bruges: Desclée De Brouwer, 1963.

Colson, Jean. *L'épiscopat catholique: collégialité et primauté dans les trois premiers siècles*. Unam Sanctam, no. 43. Paris: Cerf, 1963.

_____. *L'évêque dans les communautés primitives*. Unam Sanctam, no. 21. Paris: Cerf, 1951.

Congar, Yves M.-J. *Ministères et communion ecclésiale*. Paris: Cerf, 1971.

Congar, Yves M.-J., et al. *La collégialité épiscopale.* Unam Sanctam, no. 52. Paris: Cerf, 1965.

Congar, Yves M.-J., and Dupuy, Bernard-Dominique, eds. *L'épiscopat et l'Église universelle.* Unam Sanctam, no. 39. Paris: Cerf, 1962.

Dóriga, Enrique L. *Jerarquía, infalibilidad, y comunión intereclesial.* Barcelona: Herder, 1973.

Gagnebet, Rosarius. "De duplici subiecto unicae potestatis supremae." In *Acta congressus internationalis de theologia concilii Vaticani Secundi,* pp. 118-128. Edited by A. Schönmetzer. Vatican City: Typis Polyglottis Vaticanis, 1968.

Ghirlanda, Gianfranco. *"Hierarchica communio": significato della formula nella Lumen Gentium.* Rome: Gregoriana, 1980.

Group of Les Dombes. "The Episcopal Ministry." *One in Christ* 14 (1978): 267-288.

Lécuyer, Joseph. *Études sur la collégialité épiscopale.* Lyon: Mappus, 1964.

*McBrien, Richard. "Collegiality: The State of the Question." In *The Once and Future Church,* pp. 1-24. Edited by James A. Coriden. Staten Island, N.Y.: Alba House, 1971.

Minnerath, Roland. *Le pape: évêque universel ou premier des évêques?* Paris: Beauchesne, 1978.

Moore, Peter, ed. *Bishops but What Kind? Reflections on Episcopacy.* London: SPCK, 1982.

Mörsdorf, Klaus. "Decree on the Bishops' Pastoral Office in the Church." In *Commentary on the Documents of Vatican II*, vol. 2, 165-300. Edited by Herbert Vorgrimler. New York: Herder & Herder, 1968.

National Conference on Catholic Bishops. *The Ministry of Bishops: Papers from the Collegeville Assembly.* Washington, D.C.: USCC, 1982. (Articles by J. Dearden, J. A. Hickey, R. F. Sanchez, T. J. Gumbleton, W. D. Borders, R. G. Weakland, and G. B. Hume.)

Rahner, Karl. *Bishops: Their Status and Function.* London: Burns & Oates, 1964/ Wheathampstead: A. Clarke Books.

_____. "The Episcopal Office." In *Theological Investigations*, vol. 6, 313-360. New York: Crossroad; London: Darton, Longman & Todd, 1969. (See also similar articles in vols. 10 and 14.)

*Rahner, Karl, and Ratzinger, Joseph. *Episcopate and Primacy.* New York: Herder & Herder, 1962; London: Burns & Oates/ Wheathampstead: A. Clarke Books.

Ratzinger, Joseph. "The Pastoral Implications of Episcopal Collegiality." In *The Church and Mankind*, 39-67. Edited by Edward Schillebeeckx. Concilium, no. 1. Glen Rock, N.J.: Paulist, 1965.

Sacred Congregation for Bishops. *Directory on the Pastoral Ministry of Bishops.* Ottawa: Canadian Catholic Conference, 1974.

Schauf, Heribert. *Das Leitungsamt der Bischöfe: zur Textgeschichte der Konstitution "Lumen Gentium" des II. Vatikanischen Konzils.* Munich: F. Schöningh, 1975.

Stanley, David M. "The New Testament Basis for the Concept of Collegiality." *Theological Studies* 25 (1964): 197-216.

*Suenens, Léon Joseph. *Coresponsibility in the Church.* New York: Herder & Herder, 1968.

Swidler, Arlene, and Swidler, Leonard, eds. *Bishops and People.* Philadelphia: Westminster, 1970.

Thils, Gustave. *Primauté pontificale et prérogatives épiscopales. "Potestas ordinaria" au Concile du Vatican.* Louvain: E. Warny, 1961.

Torrell, Jean-Pierre. *La théologie de l'épiscopat au premier Concile du Vatican.* Unam Sanctam, no. 37. Paris: Cerf, 1961.

Veuillot, P., and Congar, Yves M.-J. *La charge pastorale des évêques: décret "Christus Dominus."* Unam Sanctam, no. 71. Paris: Cerf, 1969. (Articles by W. Onclin, H. Legrand, F. Boulard, and others.)

37
The Teaching Office

Alfaro, Juan. "Theology's Role Regarding the Magisterium." *Theology Digest* 25 (1977): 212-216. (Abstracted from *Gregorianum* 57 (1976): 39-79.)

Chicago Studies 17 (1978): 149-307. An entire issue is devoted to the Magisterium. (Articles by E. LaVerdiere, J. E. Lynch, Y. M.-J. Congar, A. Dulles, R. E. Brown, and others.)

Congar, Yves M.-J. "Bref historique des formes du 'magistère' et de ses relations avec les docteurs." *Revue des sciences philosophiques et théologiques* 60 (1976): 99-112, (Cf. *Theology Digest* 25/1 (1977): 15-20.) Full English version in C. E. Curran and R. A. McCormick listed below, 314-331.

Congar, Yves M.-J., et al. *Les théologiens et l'Église.* Paris: Beauchesne, 1980.

*Curran, Charles E., and McCormick, R. A., eds. *The Magisterium and Morality.* Readings in Moral Theology, no. 3. New York: Paulist, 1982.

Descamps, A. L. "Théologie et magistère." *Ephemerides theologicae lovanienses* 52 (1976): 82-133.

Dulles, Avery. "The Magisterium in History: Theological Considerations." In *A Church to Believe In*, chapter 7. New York: Crossroad, 1982.

_____. *The Resilient Church*, chapter 5. Garden City, N.Y.: Doubleday, 1977; Dublin: Gill & Macmillan, 1978.

_____. *The Survival of Dogma*. Garden City, N.Y.: Doubleday, 1971.

_____. "The Teaching Authority of the Bishops' Conferences." *America* (June 11, 1983): 453-455.

_____. "The Two Magisteria: An Interim Reflection." In *A Church to Believe In*, chapter 8. New York: Crossroad, 1982.

Empie, Paul C., Murphy, T. Austin, and Burgess, Joseph A., eds. *Teaching Authority and Infallibility in the Church*. Lutherans and Catholics in Dialogue, no. 6. Minneapolis: Augsburg, 1978.

Eno, Robert B. *Teaching Authority in the Early Church*. Wilmington, Del.: M. Glazier, 1984. (A selection of patristic texts.)

Ford, John C., and Grisez, Germain. "Contraception and the Infallibility of the Ordinary Magisterium." *Theological Studies* 39 (1978): 258-312.

International Theological Commission. *Theses on the Relationship between the Ecclesiastical Magisterium and Theology*. Washington, D.C.: USCC, 1977.

Irish Theological Quarterly 43/4 (1976): 225-292. Issue on Magisterium with articles by C. B. Daly, R. B. Coffy, K. Wojtyla, and A. Poma.

Kern, Walter, ed. *Die Theologie und das Lehramt.* Freiburg: Herder, 1982. (Articles by M. Seckler, W. Kasper, P. Eicher, and others.)

Komonchak, Joseph A. "*Humanae vitae* and its Reception: Ecclesiological Reflections." *Theological Studies* 39 (1978): 221-257.

_____. "Ordinary Papal Magisterium and Religious Assent." In *Contraception: Authority and Dissent,* pp. 101-126. Edited by C. E. Curran. New York: Herder & Herder, 1969.

McCormick, Richard A. "The Magisterium and Theologians." *Proceedings of the Catholic Theological Society of America* 24 (1969): 239-254.

McKenzie, John L. *Authority in the Church.* New York: Sheed & Ward, 1966.

Morrisey, Francis G. *The Canonical Significance of Papal and Curial Pronouncements.* Washington, D.C.: Canon Law Society of America, 1981.

O'Donovan, Leo J., ed. *Cooperation between Theologians and the Ecclesiastical Magisterium.* A Report of the Joint Committee of CLSA and CTSA. Washington, D.C.: CLSA, 1982. (Articles by J. A. Alesandro, J. P. Boyle, R. J. Carlson, P. Granfield, J. Nilson, and J. H. Provost.) This same Committee also published "Doctrinal Responsibilities: Procedures for Promoting Cooperation and Resolving Disputes between Bishops and Theologians." It is published in Canon Law Society of America, *Proceedings of the Forty-Fifth Annual Convention* (1983), 261-284, Washington, D.C.: CLSA, 1984 and *Proceedings of the Catholic Theological Society of America* 39 (1984): 209-234.

Rahner, Karl. "Magisterium." In *Sacramentum Mundi*, vol. 3, 351-358. New York: Herder & Herder, 1968. Reprinted in *Encyclopedia of Theology. The Concise Sacramentum Mundi*, pp. 871-880. New York: Seabury, 1975; Tunbridge Wells: Burns & Oates, 1975.

Recherches de science religieuse 71 (1983): 1-308. Two issues devoted to the Magisterium: "Le magistère: institution et fonctionnements." (Articles by J. Moingt, J. Doré, C. Pairault, J. Hoffmann, and others.)

Riedl, Alfons. *Die kirchliche Lehrautorität in Fragen der Moral nach den Aussagen des Ersten Vatikanischen Konzils.* Freiburg: Herder, 1979.

Sanks, T. Howland. *Authority in the Church: A Study in Changing Paradigms.* Missoula, Mont.: Scholars Press, 1974.

Seckler, Max, ed. *Lehramt und Theologie.* Düsseldorf: Patmos, 1981.

Sullivan, Francis A. "On the Infallibility of the Episcopal College in the Ordinary Exercise of its Teaching Office." In *Acta congressus internationalis de theologia concilii Vaticani Secundi*, pp. 189-195. Edited by A. Schönmetzer. Vatican City: Typis Polyglottis Vaticanis, 1968.

————. Magisterium. Teaching Office in the Catholic Church. New York: Paulist, 1983; Dublin: Gill & Macmillan, 1983.

Le Supplément, no. 133 (Mai 1980). Entire issue devoted to the Magisterium: "La régulation de la foi." (Articles by J. Guillet, A. Dumas, Y. M.-J. Congar, C. Duquoc, and others.)

Swidler, Leonard, and Fransen, Piet, eds. *Authority in the Church and the Schillebeeckx Case.* New York: Crossroad, 1982. (Articles by E. Schillebeeckx, P. Schoonenberg, T. I. Jiménez-Urresti, and others.) Also published in *Journal of Ecumenical Studies* 19/2 (1982).

Todd, John M., ed. *Problems of Authority.* Baltimore: Helicon, 1962; London: Darton, Longman & Todd, 1962.

38
Infallibility

This section lists works specifically concerned with infallibility. It is in addition to the materials found in the previous section. Some further titles are listed under Section 5: Vatican Council I.

Bantle, Franz Xaver. *Unfehlbarkeit der Kirche in Aufklärung und Romantik. Eine dogmengeschichtliche Untersuchung für die Zeit der Wende vom 18. zum 19. Jahrhundert.* Freiburg: Herder, 1976.

Butler, Basil Christopher. *The Church and Infallibility.* London: Sheed & Ward, 1954. (Rev. ed., 1969).

Castelli, Enrico, ed. *L'infallibilité: Son aspect philosophique et théologique.* Paris: Aubier, 1970.

Chirico, Peter. *Infallibility: Crossroads of Doctrine.* Kansas City: Sheed, Andrews, & McMeel, 1977; London: Sheed & Ward, 1977. (Reprinted with a foreword by B. C. Butler and a new introduction by the author. Wilmington, Del.: M. Glazier, 1983.)

De doctrina concilii Vaticani primi. Studia selecta annis 1948-1964 scripta denuo edita cum centesimus annus compleretur ab eodem inchoata concilio, pp. 285-575. Vatican City: Vaticana, 1969. Compiled by Roger Aubert and others. Contains reprints of previously published articles by J.-P. Torrell, G. Dejaifve, G. Thils, and A. Chavasse.

*Ford, John T. "Infallibility: A Review of Recent Studies." *Theological Studies* 40 (1979): 273-305.

_____. "Infallibility: Who Won the Debate?" *Proceedings of the Catholic Theological Society of America* 31 (1976): 179-192.

Goulder, M. D. *Infallibility in the Church: An Anglican-Catholic Dialogue*. London: Darton, Longman & Todd, 1968.

Horst, Ulrich. *Papst-Konzil-Unfehlbarkeit*. Mainz: Matthias-Grünewald, 1978.

_____. *Unfehlbarkeit und Geschichte. Studien zur Unfehlbarkeitsdiskussion von Melchior Cano bis zum I. Vatikanischen Konzil*. Mainz: Matthias-Grünewald, 1982.

Journal of Ecumenical Studies 8 (1971): 751-871. Devoted to infallibility. (Articles by L. Swidler, J. T. Ford, B. Tierney, and others.)

Kirvan, John J., ed. *The Infallibility Debate*. New York: Paulist, 1971.

Klausnitzer, Wolfgang. *Päpstliche Unfehlbarkeit bei Newman und Döllinger. Ein historisch-systematischer Vergleich*. Innsbruck: Tyrolia, 1980.

Küng, Hans. *Fehlbar? Eine Bilanz.* Zurich: Benziger, 1973. (Extensive bibliography on the "infallibility debate.")

_____. *Infallible? An Inquiry.* Garden City, N.Y.: Doubleday, 1971; London: Fontana, 1972.

_____. *Structures of the Church.* New York: T. Nelson, 1964; Paperback: University of Notre Dame, 1968.

Lindbeck, George A. *Infallibility.* Milwaukee: Marquette University Theology Department, 1972.

Rahner, Karl, ed. *Zum Problem Unfehlbarkeit: Antworten auf die Anfrage von Hans Küng.* Freiburg: Herder, 1971.

Rousseau, Olivier, et al. *L'infallibilité de l'Église.* Gembloux: Chevetogne, 1963.

Tekippe, Terry J., ed. *Papal Infallibility: An Application of Lonergan's Theological Method.* Washington, D.C.: University Press of America, 1983.

*Thils, Gustave. *L'infallibilité pontificale.* Gembloux: J. Duculot, 1969.

Tierney, Brian. *Origins of Papal Infallibility 1150-1350.* Leiden: Brill, 1972.

39
Councils
Ecumenical, National, and Diocesan

Botte, Bernard, et al. *Le Concile et les conciles.* Chevetogne: Chevetogne, 1960. (See especially articles by P.-T. Camelot and Y. M.-J. Congar.)

Burns, Patrick J. "Communion, Councils, and Collegiality: Some Catholic Reflections." In *Papal Primacy and the Universal Church*, pp. 151-172. Edited by P. C. Empie and T. A. Murphy. Minneapolis: Augsburg, 1974.

Congar, Yves M.-J. "The Church as an Assembly and the Church as Essentially Conciliar." In *One, Holy, Catholic, and Apostolic*, pp. 44-48. Edited by Herbert Vorgrimler. London: Sheed & Ward, 1968.

_____. "Concile." *Catholicisme*, vol. 2, pp. 1439-1443.

*_____. "La réception comme réalité ecclésiologique." *Revue des sciences philosophiques et théologiques* 56 (1972): 364-403. (See also abridged version in *Election and Consensus in the Church*, 43-68. Concilium, no. 77. Edited by Giuseppe Alberigo and Anton Weiler. New York: Herder & Herder, 1972.)

De Vries, Wilhelm. *Orient et occident. Les structures ecclé-siales vues dans l'histoire des sept premiers conciles oecuméniques.* Paris: Cerf, 1971.

Dvornik, Francis. *The Ecumenical Councils.* 20th Century Encyclopedia of Catholicism, vol. 82. New York: Hawthorn Books, 1961.

Eno, Robert B. "Pope and Council: The Patristic Origins." *Science et esprit* 28 (1976): 183-211.

*Fransen, Piet. "The Authority of the Councils." In *Problems of Authority,* pp. 43-78. Edited by John M. Todd. Baltimore: Helicon, 1962.

Grillmeier, Alois. "Konzil und Rezeption." *Theologie und Philosophie* 45 (1970): 321-352.

_____. "The Reception of Chalcedon in the Roman Catholic Church." *Ecumenical Review* 22 (1970): 383-411.

Hryniewicz, Waclaw. "Die ekklesiale Rezeption in der Sicht der orthodoxen Theologie." *Theologie und Glaube* 65 (1975): 250-266.

*Huizing, Peter, and Walf, Knut, eds. *The Ecumenical Council: Its Significance in the Constitution of the Church.* Concilium, no. 167. New York: Seabury, 1983; Edinburgh: T. & T. Clark, 1983.

Küng, Hans. *Structures of the Church.* New York: T. Nelson, 1964; Paperback: University of Notre Dame, 1968.

_____. *The Council in Action.* New York: Sheed & Ward, 1963.

Müller, Hubert. "Rezeption und Konsens in der Kirche." *Österreichisches Archiv für Kirchenrecht* 27 (1976): 3-21.

Pagé, Roch. *The Diocesan Pastoral Council.* New York: Newman, 1970.

Peri, Vittorio. *I concili e le chiese. Ricerca storica sulla tradizione d'universalità dei sinodi ecumenici.* Rome: Studium, 1965.

Schwaiger, Georg. *Päpstlicher Primat und Autorität der allgemeinen Konzilien im Spiegel der Geschichte.* Paderborn: F. Schöningh, 1977.

Sieben, Hermann-Josef. *Die Konzilsidee der Alten Kirche.* Paderborn: F. Schöningh, 1979.

United States Catholic Conference. *A National Pastoral Council: Pro and Con.* Washington, D.C.: USCC, 1971.

40
The Synod of Bishops and
The Episcopal Conference

Antón, Angel. *Primado y colegialidad. Sus relaciones a la luz del primer Sínodo extraordinario.* Madrid: Católica, 1970.

Congar, Yves M.-J. "Synode épiscopal, primauté et collegialité épiscopale." In *Ministères et communion ecclésiale,* pp. 187-227. Paris: Cerf, 1981.

Dvornik, Francis. "Origins of Episcopal Synods." In *The Once and Future Church,* pp. 25-56. Edited by James A. Coriden. Staten Island, N.Y.: Alba House, 1971.

Fagiolo, Vincenzo. "Il synodus episcoporum: origine, natura, struttura, compiti." In *La collegialità episcopale per il futuro della chiesa,* pp. 3-43. Edited by Vincenzo Fagiola and Gino Concetti. Florence: Vallechi, 1969.

Feliciani, Giorgio. *Le conferenze episcopali.* Bologna: Il Mulino, 1974.

Fesquet, Henri. *Le synode et l'avenir de l'Église.* Paris: Centurion, 1972.

Las conferencias episcopales hoy. Actas del simposio de 1-3 Mayo, 1975. Salamanca: Universidad Pontificia, 1977.

Laurentin, René. *L'enjeu du synode, suite du concile.* Paris: Seuil, 1967.

_____. *Le premier synode: histoire et bilan.* Paris: Seuil, 1968.

_____. *Enjeu du deuxième synode et contestation dans l'Église.* Paris: Seuil, 1969.

_____. *Le synode permanent: naissance et avenir.* Paris: Seuil, 1970.

_____. *Réorientation de l'Église après le IIIe synode.* Paris: Seuil, 1972.

_____. *L'évangélisation après le IV synode.* Paris: Seuil, 1975.

*Legrand, Hervé-M. "Synodes et conciles de l'après-concile. Quelques enjeux ecclésiologiques." *Nouvelle revue théologique* 98 (1976): 193-216.

Lettmann, Reinhard. "Episcopal Conferences in the New Canon Law." *Studia Canonica* 14 (1980): 347-367.

McManus, Frederick. "The Scope of Authority of Episcopal Conferences." In *The Once and Future Church*, pp. 129-178. Edited by James A. Coriden. Staten Island, N.Y.: Alba House, 1971.

Murphy, Francis X., and MacEoin, Gary. *Synod of '67: A New Sound in Rome.* Milwaukee: Bruce, 1968.

Price, Bernard. "Episcopal Conferences and Collegiality." *Studia Canonica* 2 (1968): 125-132.

41
The Particular or The Local Church

Allmen, Jean Jacques von. "L'Église locale parmi les autres églises locales." *Irénikon* 43 (1970): 512-537.

Amato, Angelo, ed., *La chiesa locale.* Rome: Libreria Ateneo Salesiano, 1976.

Bazatole, B. "L'évêque et la vie chrétienne au sein de l'Église locale." In *L'épiscopat et l'Église universelle*, 329-360. Edited by Y. Congar and B.-D. Dupuy. Paris: Cerf, 1962.

Beinert, Wolfgang. "Dogmenhistorische Anmerkungen zum Begriff 'Partikularkirche'." *Theologie une Philosophie* 50 (1975): 38-69.

——————. "Die Kirche Christi als Lokalkirche." *Una Sancta* 32 (1977): 114-129.

Contri, Antonio. *La teologia della chiesa locale e i suoi orientamenti fondamentali.* Rome: Urbaniana, 1974.

Curran, Charles E., and Dyer, George J., eds. *Shared Responsibility in the Local Church.* Chicago: Chicago Studies, 1970.

Dortel-Claudot, Michel. *Églises locales — Église universelle. Comment se gouverne le peuple de Dieu.* Lyon: Le Chalet, 1973.

Ernst, Josef. "From the Local Community to the Great Church, Illustrated from the Church Patterns of Philippians and Ephesians." *Biblical Theology Bulletin* 6 (1976): 237-257.

Lanne, Emmanuel. "The Local Church: Its Catholicity and Its Apostolicity." *One in Christ* 6 (1970): 288-313.

Legrand, Hervé-M. "La réalisation de l'Église en un lieu." In *Initiation à la pratique de la théologie*, vol. 3, 143-345. Edited by B. Lauret and F. Refoulé. Paris: Cerf, 1983.

_____. "The Revaluation of Local Churches: Some Theological Implications." In *The Unifying Role of the Bishop*, 53-64. Edited by Edward Schillebeeckx. Concilium, no. 71. New York: Herder & Herder, 1972.

*Lubac, Henri de. *The Motherhood of the Church, followed by Particular Churches in the Universal Church.* San Francisco: Ignatius, 1982.

Neunheuser, Burkhard. "Église universelle et Église locale." In *L'Église de Vatican II*, vol. 2, 607-638. Edited by G. Baraúna. 3 vols. Unam Sanctam, no. 51 a, b, and c. Paris: Cerf, 1966. (Italian version: *La Chiesa del Vaticano II.* Florence: Vallecchi, 1965. German version: *De Ecclesia: Beiträge zur Konstitution über die Kirche des II. Vatikanischen Konzils.* Freiburg: Herder, 1966.)

O'Rourke, John J. "The Office of Bishop and its Relationship to the Particular Churches and to the United States." *Studia Canonica* 5 (1971): 227-244.

* *Proceedings of the Catholic Theological Society of America* 35 (1980). (Articles on local church by P. Granfield, S. Kilian, F. Parrella, B. Prusak.)

* *Proceedings of the Catholic Theological Society of America* 36 (1981). (Articles on local church by R. E. Brown, M. Fahey, J. Komonchak, et al.)

Schick, Edward. "Importance of the Local Church." In *Council Speeches of Vatican II*, pp. 35-38. Edited by Hans Küng et al. Glen Rock, N.J.: Paulist Deus Books, 1964.

Tessarolo, Andrea, ed. *La chiesa locale.* Bologna: Dehoniane, 1970.

World Council of Churches. *In Each Place: Towards a Fellowship of Local Churches Truly United.* Geneva: WCC, 1977.

Zbignievus, Joseph T. *Actualisatio ecclesiae universalis in ecclesia locali iuxta Concilii Vaticani II.* Rome: Angelicum, 1970.

42
The Parish

The following authors apply the theology of the local Church to the parish.

Arnold, Franz Xaver, et al. *Handbuch der Pastoraltheologie,* vol. 3, 111-262. Freiburg: Herder, 1968. (Articles by N. Greinacher, A. Müller, R. Fischer-Wollpert, and others.)

*Blöchlinger, Alex. *The Modern Parish Community.* New York: P. J. Kenedy, 1965.

Bordelon, Marvin, ed. *The Parish in a Time of Change.* Notre Dame, Ind.: Fides, 1967.

Connan, Francis, and Barreau, Jean Claude. *Demain, la paroisse.* Paris: Seuil, 1966.

Davis, Charles. "The Parish and Theology." *Clergy Review* 49 (1964): 265-290.

Downs, Thomas. *The Parish as Learning Community.* New York: Paulist, 1979.

Floristan, Casiano. *The Parish — Eucharistic Community.* Notre Dame: Fides, 1964.

Geaney, Dennis J. *The Prophetic Parish: A Center for Peace and Justice.* Minneapolis: Winston, 1983.

Greeley, Andrew M., et al. *Parish, Priest, and People.* Chicago: Thomas More, 1981.

*Kilian, Sabbas J. *Theological Models for the Parish.* Staten Island, N.Y.: Alba House, 1977.

Michonneau, Georges. *Revolution in a City Parish.* Westminster, Md.: Newman, 1949.

National Conference of Catholic Bishops. *The Parish: A People, A Mission, A Structure.* Washington, D.C.: USCC, 1980.

National Conference of Catholic Bishops. *Parish Life in the United States. Final Report to the Bishops of the United States by the Parish Project.* Washington, D.C.: USCC, 1983.

Newsome, Robert R. *The Ministering Parish: Methods and Procedures for the Pastoral Organization.* New York: Paulist, 1982.

O'Gara, James, ed. *The Postconciliar Parish.* New York: P. J. Kenedy, 1967.

Quinn, Bernard. *The Small Rural Parish.* Washington, D.C.: Glenmary Research Center, 1980.

*Rahner, Hugo, ed. *The Parish from Theology to Practice.* Westminster, Md.: Newman, 1958.

Roy, Paul S. *Building Christian Communities for Justice.* New York: Paulist, 1981.

Searle, Mark, ed. *Parish: A Place for Worship.* Collegeville, Minn.: Liturgical, 1981.

Sweetser, Thomas. *Successful Parishes: How They Meet the Challenge of Peace.* Minneapolis: Winston, 1983.

Whitehead, Evelyn E., ed. *The Parish in Community and Ministry.* New York: Paulist, 1978.

Whitehead, Evelyn E., and Whitehead, James D. *Community of Faith. Models and Strategies for Developing Christian Communities.* New York: Seabury, 1973.

43
Charisms in the Church

Agrimson, J. Elmo, ed. *Gifts of the Spirit and the Body of Christ: Perspectives on the Charismatic Movement.* Minneapolis: Augsburg, 1974.

*Congar, Yves M.-J. *I Believe in the Holy Spirit*, vol. 2, 147-201. New York: Seabury, 1983.

Cullmann, Oscar. "La notion biblique du charisme et l'oecuménisme." *Revue thomiste* 71 (1971): 520-527.

Culpepper, Robert H. *Evaluating the Charismatic Movement: A Theological and Biblical Appraisal.* Valley Forge, Pa.: Judson, 1977.

Duquoc, Christian, and Floristan, Casiano, eds. *Charisms in the Church.* Concilium, no. 109. New York: Seabury, 1978.

Fahey, Sheila M. *Charismatic Social Action.* New York: Paulist, 1977.

Fichter, Joseph. *The Catholic Cult of the Paraclete.* New York: Sheed & Ward, 1975.

Gelpi, Donald. *Charism and Sacrament: A Theology of Christian Conversion.* New York: Paulist, 1976.

Hassenhüttl, Gotthold. *Charisma: Ordnungsprinzip der Kirche.* Freiburg: Herder, 1969.

Hollenweger, Walter J. *The Pentecostals: The Charismatic Movement in the Churches.* Minneapolis: Augsburg, 1972.

Jones, J. *Filled with New Wine: The Charismatic Renewal of the Church.* New York: Seabury, 1976.

Küng, Hans. "The Charismatic Structure of the Church." In *Pastoral Reform in Church Government,* 41-61. Concilium, no. 8. Edited by Neophytos Edelby and Teodoro Jiménez-Urresti. Glen Rock, N.J.: Paulist, 1965.

McDonnell, Kilian. *Charismatic Renewal and the Churches.* New York: Seabury, 1976.

_____. *The Charismatic Renewal and Ecumenism.* New York: Paulist, 1978.

_____, ed. *The Holy Spirit and Power.* Garden City, N.Y.: Doubleday, 1975.

_____, ed. *Presence, Power, Praise: Documents on the Charismatic Renewal.* 3 vols. Collegeville, Minn.: Liturgical, 1980.

Mühlen, Heribert. *A Charismatic Theology: Initiation in the Spirit.* New York: Paulist, 1978.

Quebedeaux, Richard. *The New Charismatics II.* San Francisco: Harper & Row, 1983.

*Rahner, Karl. *The Dynamic Element in the Church.* New York: Herder & Herder, 1964.

Schürmann, Heinz. "Les charismes spirituels." In *L'Église de Vatican II*, vol. 2, 541-573. Edited by G. Baraúna. 3 vols. Unam Sanctam, no. 51 a, b, and c. Paris: Cerf, 1966. (Italian version: *La Chiesa del Vaticano II.* Florence: Vallecchi, 1965. German version: *De Ecclesia: Beiträge zur Konstitution über die Kirche des II. Vatikanischen Konzils.* Freiburg: Herder, 1966.)

Suenens, Léon Joseph. *A New Pentecost?* New York: Seabury, 1975; London: Fount Publications, 1977.

*Sullivan, Francis A. *Charisms and Charismatic Renewal: A Biblical and Theological Study.* Ann Arbor: Servant, 1982; Dublin: Gill & Macmillan, 1982.

Theological and Pastoral Orientations on the Charismatic Renewal. Prepared at Malines, Belgium. Notre Dame, Ind.: Communication Center, 1974.

44
Ordained Ministers in the Church

Balthasar, Hans Urs von. "Office in the Church." In *Church and World*, chapter 2, pp. 44-111. New York: Herder & Herder, 1967.

Burrows, William R. *New Ministries: The Global Context.* Maryknoll, N.Y.: Orbis, 1980.

*Congar, Yves M.-J. *Ministères et communion ecclésiale.* Paris: Cerf, 1971.

Cooke, Bernard. *Ministry to Word and Sacraments.* Philadelphia: Fortress, 1976.

Cordes, Paul J. *Sendung zum Dienst. Exegetisch-historische und systematische Studien zum Konzilsdekret "vom Dienst und Leben der Priester."* Frankfurt: J. Knecht, 1972.

Delorme, Jean. *Le ministère et les ministères selon le Nouveau Testament.* Paris: Seuil, 1974.

Grollenberg, Lucas, et al. *Minister? Pastor? Prophet? Grassroots Leadership in the Church.* New York:

Crossroad, 1981. (Articles by J. Kerkhofs, A. Houtepen, J. J. A. Vollebergh, and E. Schillebeeckx.)

Hastings, Adrian. *Church and Ministry.* Kampala: Gaba, 1972.

Iersel, Bas van, and Murphy, Roland, eds. *Office and Ministry in the Church.* Concilium, no. 80. New York: Herder & Herder, 1972.

Lécuyer, Joseph, et al. "Decree on the Ministry and Life of Priests." In *Commentary on the Documents of Vatican II*, vol. 4, 183-297. Edited by Herbert Vorgrimler. New York: Herder & Herder, 1969.

Lemaire, André. *Les ministères aux origines de l'Église — Naissance de la triple hierarchie: évêques, presbytres, diacres.* Paris: Cerf, 1971.

Lienhard, Joseph T. *Ministry.* Wilmington, Del.: M. Glazier, 1984. (A selection of patristic texts.)

Mitchell, Nathan. *Mission and Ministry: History and Theology in the Sacrament of Order.* Wilmington, Del.: M. Glazier, 1982.

Mohler, James A. *The Origin and Evolution of the Priesthood.* Staten Island, N.Y.: Alba House, 1970.

Niebuhr, H. Richard. *The Purpose of the Church and its Ministry.* New York: Harper, 1956.

Neuhaus, Richard John. *Freedom for Ministry: A Critical Affirmation of the Church and its Mission.* San Francisco/London: Harper & Row, 1979.

Nowell, Robert. *The Ministry of Service: Deacons in the Contemporary Church.* New York: Herder & Herder, 1968.

O'Meara, Thomas F. *Theology and Ministry.* New York: Paulist, 1983.

Power, David N. *The Christian Priest: Elder and Prophet.* London: Sheed & Ward, 1973.

——————. *Ministers of Christ and His Church. The Theology of Priesthood.* London: G. Chapman, 1969.

*Provost, James H., ed. *Official Ministry in a New Age.* Washington, D.C.: Canon Law Society of America, 1981. (Articles by J. H. Provost, C. Osiek, J. Komonchak, and others.)

Schillebeeckx, Edward. "The Catholic Understanding of Office in the Church." *Theological Studies* 30 (1969): 567-587. (Reprinted in his *Mission of the Church*, pp. 205-228. New York: Seabury, 1973; London: Sheed & Ward, 1981.)

——————. *Ministry. Leadership in the Community of Jesus.* New York: Crossroad, 1981.

Tavard, George H. *A Theology for Ministry.* Wilmington, Del.: M. Glazier, 1983.

Vilela, Albano. *La condition collégiale des prêtres du IIIe siècle.* Paris: Beauchesne, 1971.

Wasselynck, René. *Les prêtres. Elaboration du décret Presbyterorum ordinis de Vatican II.* Paris: Desclée, 1968.

Whitehead, Evelyn Eaton, and Whitehead, James D. *Method in Ministry.* New York: Seabury, 1981.

Winninger, Paul, and Congar, Yves M.-J., eds. *Le diacre dans l'Église et le monde d'aujourd'hui.* Unam Sanctam, no. 59. Paris: Cerf, 1966.

45
Religious in the Church

Balthasar, Hans Urs von. *The Christian State of Life.* San Francisco: Ignatius, 1983.

Beyer, Jean. *Religious Life or Secular Institute?* Rome: Gregoriana, 1970.

*Cada, Lawrence, et al. *Shaping of the Coming Age of Religious Life.* New York: Seabury, 1979.

Clarke, Thomas E. *New Pentecost or New Passion? The Directions of Religious Life Today.* New York: Paulist, 1973.

Cussiánovich, Alejandro. *Religious Life and the Poor: Liberation Theology Perspective.* Maryknoll, N.Y.: Orbis, 1979; Dublin: Gill & Macmillan, 1979.

Daly, Robert J., et al. *Religious Life in the U.S. Church: The New Dialogue.* New York: Paulist, 1984. (Articles by J. R. Quinn, J. Hennesey, J. W. Padberg, E. McDonough, and others.)

Dyer, Ralph J. *The New Religious: An Authentic Life.* Milwaukee: Bruce, 1971.

Gelpi, Donald L. *Discerning the Spirit: Foundations and Futures of Religious Life.* New York: Sheed & Ward, 1970.

Huizing, Peter, and Bassett, William, eds. *The Future of Religious Life.* Concilium, no. 97. New York: Herder & Herder, 1974-75.

Huyghe, Gérard, et al. *Religious Orders in the Modern World.* Westminster, Md.: Newman, 1965. (Articles by K. Rahner, J. Hamer, J. Urtasun, and others.)

Kolmer, Elizabeth. *Religious Women in the United States: A Survey of the Influential Literature from 1950 to 1983.* Wilmington, Del.: M. Glazier, 1984.

*Lozano, John M. *Discipleship: Toward an Understanding of Religious Life.* Second edition. Chicago: Claret Center for Resources in Spirituality, 1983.

Maloney, Francis. *A Life of Promise: Poverty, Chastity, Obedience.* Wilmington, Del.: M. Glazier, 1984.

Martelet, Gustave. *The Church's Holiness and Religious Life.* St. Marys, Kan.: Review for Religious, 1966.

Moran, Gabriel, and Harris, Maria. *Experiences in Community. Should Religious Life Survive?* New York: Herder & Herder, 1968.

Neal, Marie Augusta. *Catholic Sisters in Transition: From the 1960's to the 1980's.* Wilmington, Del.: M. Glazier, 1984.

*Orsy, Ladislas M. *Open to the Spirit. Religious Life after Vatican II.* Washington, D.C.: Corpus, 1968.

Tillard, Jean M. R. *Devant Dieu et pour le monde. Le projet des religieux.* Paris: Desclée De Brouwer, 1966.

Tillard, J. M. R., and Congar, Yves M.-J., eds. *L'adaptation et la rénovation de la vie religieuse: décret "Perfectae caritatis."* Unam Sanctam, no. 62. Paris: Cerf, 1967.

Wulf, Friedrich. "Decree on the Appropriate Renewal of the Religious Life." In *Commentary on the Documents of Vatican II*, vol. 2, 301-370. Edited by Herbert Vorgrimler. New York: Herder & Herder, 1968.

46
The Laity in the Church

Barta, Russell, ed. *Challenge to the Laity*. Huntington, Ind.: Our Sunday Visitor, 1980. (Contains the text of the Chicago Declaration of Christian Concern and articles by E. Marciniak, M. Novak, J. Coleman, and S. Shriver.)

Boff, Leonardo. *God's Witnesses in the Heart of the World*. Chicago: Claret Center for Resources in Spirituality, 1981.

Collins, Mary, and Power, David, eds. *Can We Always Celebrate the Eucharist?* Concilium, no. 152. New York: Seabury, 1982; Edinburgh: T. & T. Clark, 1982.

*Congar, Yves M.-J. *Lay People in the Church*. Westminster, Md.: Newman, 1957.

_____. *Laity, Church, and World*. Baltimore: Helicon, 1960.

_____. *Ministères et communion ecclésiale*. Paris: Cerf, 1971. Chapter 1 is also in English: "My Pathfindings in the Theology of the Laity." *The Jurist* 32 (1972): 169-188.

Dabin, Paul. *Le sacerdoce royal des fidèles dans les livres saints.* Paris: Bloud, 1941.

_____. *Le sacerdoce royal des fidèles dans la tradition ancienne et moderne.* Brussels: Desclée De Brouwer, 1950.

Del Portillo, Alvaro. *Faithful and Laity in the Church.* Shannon, Ireland: Ecclesia, 1972.

Doohan, Leonard. *The Lay-Centered Church: Theology and Spirituality.* Minneapolis: Winston, 1984.

Fenhagen, James. *Mutual Ministry.* New York: Seabury, 1977.

Goldie, Rosemary. "Laity: A Bibliographical Survey of Three Decades." *The Laity Today* 26 (1979): 107-143.

International Congress on the Lay Apostolate. *L'apostolato dei laici. Bibliografia sistematica.* Milan. Vita e Pensiero, 1957. (Bibliography on the laity from 1922 to 1957.)

Klostermann, Ferdinand. "Der Apostolat der Laier in der Kirche." In *Handbuch der Pastoraltheologie*, vol. 3, 586-635. Edited by Franz Xaver Arnold, et al. Freiburg: Herder, 1968.

*_____. "Decree on the Apostolate of the Laity." In *Commentary on the Documents of Vatican II*, vol. 3, 273-404. Edited by Herbert Vorgrimler. New York: Herder & Herder, 1969. (See also vol. 1, 231-252.)

National Conference on Catholic Bishops. *Called and Gifted.* Washington, D.C.: USCC, 1980.

_____. *To Build and Be Church.* Washington, D.C.: USCC, 1979.

O'Gara, James, ed. *The Layman in the Church.* New York: Herder & Herder, 1962. (Articles by J. T. Ellis, R. W. Hovda, J. G. Lawler, and others.)

Peck, George, and Hoffman, John S., eds. *The Laity in Ministry: The Whole People of God for the Whole World.* Valley Forge, Pa.: Judson, 1984.

Philips, Gérard. *Achieving Christian Maturity.* Chicago: Franciscan Herald, 1966.

_____. *The Role of the Laity in the Church.* Chicago: Fides, 1956.

*Power, David N. *Gifts that Differ. Lay Ministries Established and Unestablished.* New York: Pueblo, 1980.

Pro Mundi Vita 62 (1976): New Forms of Ministry in Christian Communities.

Rahner, Karl. "Notes on the Lay Apostolate." In *Theological Investigations,* vol. 2, 219-352. New York: Crossroad; London: Darton, Longman & Todd, 1963. (See also other articles on the laity in vols. 3 and 8 of *Theological Investigations.*)

Schillebeeckx, Edward. "The Typological Definition of the Christian Laymen according to Vatican II." In *The Mission of the Church,* pp. 90-117. New York: Seabury, 1973; London: Sheed & Ward, 1981.

47
Women in the Church

Bouyer, Louis. *Woman in the Church.* San Francisco: Ignatius, 1979.

*Butler, Sara, ed. *Research Report: Women in Church and Society.* Mahwah, N.J.: Catholic Theological Society of America, 1978.

Chittister, Joan. *Women, Ministry, and the Church.* New York: Paulist, 1983.

Clark, Elizabeth A. *Women in the Early Church.* Wilmington, Del.: M. Glazier, 1983.

*Elizondo, Virgil, and Greinacher, Norbert, eds. *Women in a Man's Church.* Concilium, no. 134. New York: Seabury, 1980.

Ermath,.Margaret Sittler. *Adam's Fractured Rib: Observations on Women in the Church.* Philadelphia: Fortress, 1970.

Fiorenza, Elisabeth S. *In Memory of Her.* New York: Crossroad, 1983; London: SCM, 1983.

Galot, Jean. *L'Église et la femme.* Gembloux: J. Duculot, 1965.

Gryson, Roger. *The Ministry of Women in the Early Church.* Collegeville, Minn.: Liturgical, 1976.

Harkness, Georgia Elma. *Women in Church and Society: A Historical and Theological Inquiry.* Nashville: Abingdon, 1972.

Laflaive, Anne. *La femme et l'Église.* Paris: France-Empire. 1968.

Moltmann-Wendel, Elizabeth. *Liberty, Equality, Sisterhood: On the Emancipation of Women in Church and Society.* Philadelphia: Fortress, 1978.

Ruether, Rosemary Radford, ed. *Religion and Sexism: Images of Women in the Jewish and Christian Tradition.* New York: Simon and Schuster, 1974.

Russell, Letty M. *Human Liberation in a Feminist Perspective: A Theology.* Philadelphia: Westminster, 1974.

Swidler, Leonard, and Swidler, Arlene, eds. *Women Priests: A Catholic Commentary on the Vatican Declaration.* New York: Paulist, 1977.

Tavard, George H. *Woman in Christian Tradition.* Notre Dame: Ind.: University of Notre Dame, 1973.

48
The "Sense of the Faithful"

This section presupposes the literature presented in Sections 43-47.

Congar, Yves M.-J. "Quod omnes tangit, ab omnibus tractari et approbari debet." *Revue historique de droit français et étranger* 35 (1958): 210-259.

_____. "The 'Sensus Fidelium' in the Fathers." In *Lay People in the Church*, pp. 441-443. Westminster, Md.: Newman, 1957.

_____. *Tradition and Traditions*, pp. 314-338. New York: Macmillan, 1966.

Eno, Robert B. "Consensus and Doctrine: Three Ancient Views." *Église et théologie* 9 (1978): 473-483.

Femiano, Samuel D. *Infallibility of the Laity: The Legacy of Newman*. New York: Herder & Herder, 1967.

Ford, John T. "Newman on 'Sensus Fidelium' and Mariology." *Marian Studies* 28 (1977): 120-147.

Granfield, Patrick. "Concilium and Consensus: Decision-Making in Cyprian." *The Jurist* 35 (1975): 397-408.

_____. "Episcopal Elections in Cyprian: Clerical and Lay Participation." *Theological Studies* 37 (1976): 41-52.

King, Geoffrey. "The Acceptance of Law by the Community: A Study in the Writings of Canonists and Theologians, 1500-1750." *The Jurist* 37 (1977): 233-265.

*Newman, John Henry. *On Consulting the Faithful in Matters of Doctrine.* Reprinted with an introduction by J. Coulson. New York: Sheed & Ward, 1962.

Osawa, Takeo. *Das Bischofseinsetzungsverfahren bei Cyprian. Historische Untersuchungen zu den Begriffen iudicium, suffragium, testimonium, consensus.* Bern/Frankfurt: P. Lang, 1983.

Sesboüé, Bernard. "Autorité de magistère et vie de foi ecclésiale." *Nouvelle revue théologique* 93 (1971): 337-362.

Thils, Gustave. *L'Infaillibilité du peuple chrétien in credendo: notes de théologie posttridentine.* Paris: Desclée De Brouwer, 1963.

Thompson, William M. "*Sensus Fidelium* and Infallibility." *American Ecclesiastical Review* 167 (1973): 450-486.

*Tillard, Jean M. R. "*Sensus fidelium.*" *One in Christ* 11 (1975): 2-29.

49
The Church in the World:
The Social Mission of the Church

Arnold, Franz Xaver, Rahner, Karl, et al. *Handbuch der Pastoraltheologie.* vol. II/2. Freiburg: Herder, 1966. (See especially the contributions of K. Rahner and J. B. Metz.)

Auer, Alfons, et al. *The Christian and the World: Readings in Theology.* New York: P. J. Kenedy. 1965.

Benestad, J. Brian. *The Pursuit of a Just Social Order: Policy Statements of the U.S. Catholic Bishops.* Washington, D.C.: Ethics and Public Policy Center, 1982.

Berger, Peter L., and Neuhaus, Richard John, eds. *Against the World for the World.* New York: Seabury, 1976.

Clarke, Thomas E., ed. *Above Every Name: The Lordship of Christ and Social Systems.* New York: Paulist, 1980. (Articles by M. K. Hellwig, A. Dulles, F. Cardman, J. Farrelly, and others.)

Cosmao, Vincent. *Changing the Church: An Agenda for the Churches.* Maryknoll, N.Y.: Orbis, 1984.

Cushing, Richard Cardinal. Pastoral Letter. *The Servant Church*. Boston: Daughters of St. Paul, 1966.

*Fiorenza, Francis S. *Foundational Theology: Jesus and the Church*, chapters 7 and 8. New York: Crossroad, 1984.

Gremillion, Joseph, ed. *The Gospel of Peace and Justice: Catholic Social Teaching since Pope John*. Maryknoll, N.Y.: Orbis, 1976.

Haughey, John C., ed. *The Faith that Does Justice: Examining the Christian Sources for Social Change*. New York: Paulist, 1977. (Articles by A. Dulles, J. P. Langan, D. Hollenbach, and others.)

Hengel, Martin. *Property and Riches in the Early Church*. Philadelphia: Fortress, 1974.

Marty, Martin E. *The Public Church*. New York: Crossroad: 1981.

Metz, John B. *The Emergent Church*. New York: Crossroad, 1981; London: SCM, 1981.

_____. *Faith in History and Society*. New York: Seabury, 1980; Tunbridge Wells: Burns & Oates, 1980.

*_____. *Theology of the World*. New York: Herder & Herder, 1969; Tunbridge Wells: Search Press, 1969.

_____, ed. *The Church and the World*. Concilium, no. 6. Glen Rock, N.J.: Paulist, 1965.

O'Brien, David J., and Shannon, Thomas A., eds. *Renewing the Earth: Documents on Peace, Justice, and Lib-*

eration. Garden City, N.Y.: Doubleday Image, 1977; London: Doubleday & Co., 1977.

Rahner, Karl. "Church and World." In *Sacramentum Mundi*, vol. 1, 346-357. New York: Herder & Herder, 1968. Reprinted in *Encyclopedia of Theology: The Concise Sacramentum Mundi*, pp. 237-250. New York: Seabury, 1975; Tunbridge Wells: Burns & Oates, 1975.

Ramsey, Paul. *Who Speaks for the Church?* Nashville: Abingdon, 1967.

Ratzinger, Joseph, Semmelroth, Otto, et al. "Pastoral Constitution on the Church in the Modern World." In *Commentary on the Documents of Vatican II*, vol. 5. Edited by Herbert Vorgrimler. New York: Herder & Herder, 1969. (See especially, Yves M.-J. Congar, "The Role of the Church in the Modern World," 202-223.)

Ryle, Edward, ed. *The Social Mission of the Church: A Theological Reflection.* Washington, D.C.: Catholic University of America, 1972.

Schillebeeckx, Edward. *God the Future of Man.* New York: Sheed & Ward, 1968; London: Sheed & Ward, 1977.

_____. *The Mission of the Church.* New York: Seabury, 1973; London: Sheed & Ward, 1981.

_____. *World and Church.* New York: Sheed & Ward, 1971; London: Sheed & Ward, 1982.

Yoder, John Howard. *The Politics of Jesus.* Grand Rapids: W. B. Eerdmans, 1972.

50
Liberation Ecclesiology

This section does not give a complete listing of the theology of liberation. We have selected those works that have specific ecclesiological content.

Assmann, Hugo. *Theology for a Nomad Church.* Maryknoll, N.Y.: Orbis, 1976.

Balasuriya, Tissa. *The Eucharist and Human Liberation.* Maryknoll, N.Y.: Orbis, 1977; London, SCM, 1979.

Between Honesty and Hope: Documents from and about the Church in Latin America. Maryknoll, N.Y.: Orbis, 1976.

Boff, Leonardo. *Igreja: Carisma e poder.* Petrópolis, RJ, Brazil: Vozes, 1981. (English translation in production.)

*Brown, Robert McAfee. *Theology in a New Key: Responding to Liberation Themes.* Philadelphia: Westminster, 1978.

Cone, James H. *A Black Theology of Liberation.* Philadelphia, Lippincott, 1970.

_____. *God of the Oppressed.* New York: Seabury, 1975.

_____. *For My People: Black Theology and the Black Church.* Maryknoll, N.Y.: Orbis, 1984.

*Congregation for the Doctrine of the Faith. "Instruction on Certain Aspects of the Theology of Liberation." *Origins* (Sept. 13, 1984): 193-204.

Davies, John G. *Christians, Politics and Violent Revolution.* Maryknoll, N.Y.: Orbis, 1976.

Dussel, Enrique. *History and the Theology of Liberation.* Maryknoll, N.Y.: Orbis, 1976.

_____. *A History of the Church in Latin America: Colonialism to Liberation (1492-1979).* Grand Rapids: W. B. Eerdmans, 1982.

Eagleson, John, and Scharper, Philip. *Puebla and Beyond.* Maryknoll, N.Y.: Orbis, 1979.

Elizondo, Virgil, and Greinacher, Norbert, eds. *Tensions between the Churches of the First World and the Third World.* Concilium, no. 144. New York: Seabury, 1981.

Gardiner, James J., and Roberts, J. Deotis, eds. *Quest for a Black Theology.* Philadelphia: Fortress, 1974.

Gibellini, Rosino, ed. *Frontiers of Theology in Latin America.* Maryknoll, N.Y.: Orbis, 1979.

*Gutiérrez, Gustavo. *A Theology of Liberation.* Maryknoll, N.Y.: Orbis, 1973; London: SCM, 1974.

Gutiérrez, Gustavo, and Schaull, R. *Liberation and Change.* Atlanta: J. Knox, 1977.

Hennelly, Alfred T. "Theological Method: The Southern Exposure." *Theological Studies* 38 (1977): 709-735.

_____. *Theologies in Conflict: The Challenge of Juan Luis Segundo.* Maryknoll, N.Y.: Orbis, 1979.

International Theological Commission. "Human Development and Christian Salvation." *Origins* 7 (Nov. 3, 1977): 305-313.

Kloppenburg, Bonaventure. *The People's Church.* Chicago: Franciscan Herald, 1978.

Latin American Episcopal Council (CELAM). *The Church in the Present-Day Transformation of Latin America in the Light of the Council: Conclusions.* (The Medellín Conference.) Bogotá: General Secretariat of CELAM, 1970.

_____. *III General Conference of Latin American Bishops, Evangelization at Present and in the Future of Latin America.* (The Puebla Conference.) Washington, D.C.: NCCB, 1979.

Laurentin, René. *Liberation, Development, and Salvation.* Maryknoll, N.Y.: Orbis, 1972.

McCann, Dennis. *Christian Realism and Liberation Theology: Practical Theologies in Creative Conflict.* Maryknoll, N.Y.: Orbis, 1981.

McGovern, Arthur F. *Marxism: An American Christian Perspective.* Maryknoll, N.Y.: Orbis, 1980.

Mahan, Brian, and Richesin, L. Dale, eds. *The Challenge of Liberation Theology: A First World Response.* Maryknoll, N.Y.: Orbis, 1981.

Miguez Bonino, José. *Doing Theology in a Revolutionary Situation.* Philadelphia: Fortress, 1975.

Novak, Michael, ed. *Liberation South, Liberation North.* Washington, D.C.: American Enterprise Institute, 1981.

Ogden, Schubert M. *Faith and Freedom. Towards a Theology of Liberation.* Nashville: Abingdon, 1979; Belfast: Christian Journals, 1979.

Quade, Quentin L., ed. *The Pope and Revolution: John Paul II Confronts Liberation Theology.* Washington, D.C.: Ethics and Public Policy Center, 1982.

Ruether, Rosemary. *Liberation Theology.* New York: Paulist, 1972.

Sanks, T. Howland, and Smith, Brian H. "Liberation Ecclesiology." *Theological Studies* 38 (1977): 3-38.

Schall, James V. *Liberation Theology in Latin America.* San Francisco: Ignatius, 1982.

Segundo, Juan Luis. *Faith and Ideologies.* Maryknoll, N.Y.: Orbis, 1984.

_____. *The Hidden Motives of Pastoral Action.* Maryknoll, N.Y.: Orbis, 1978.

_____. *The Liberation of Theology.* Maryknoll, N.Y.: Orbis, 1976.

*_____. *A Theology for Artisans of a New Humanity.* vol. 1: *The Community Called Church.* Maryknoll, N.Y.: Orbis, 1973; Dublin: Gill & Macmillan, 1973.

Sobrino, Jon. *The True Church and the Poor.* Maryknoll, N.Y.: Orbis, 1984.

Torres, Sergio, and Eagleson, John, eds. *Theology in the Americas.* Maryknoll, N.Y.: Orbis, 1976.

51
The Church, the Kingdom, and the Eschaton

Bright, John. *Kingdom of God: The Biblical Concept and Its Meaning for the Church*. Nashville: Abingdon, 1953. (Reprinted under title: *The Kingdom of God in Bible and Church*. London: Lutterworth, 1955.)

Corell, Alf. *Consummatum est. Eschatology and Church in the Gospel of John*. London: SPCK, 1958.

Cullmann, Oscar. "The Kingship of Christ and the Church in the New Testament." In *The Early Church*, pp. 105-137. Philadelphia: Westminster, 1956.

Dulles, Avery. "The Church as Eschatological Community." In *The Eschaton: A Community of Love*, vol. 4, 69-103. Edited by J. Papin. Villanova University Symposium. Philadelphia: Villanova University, 1971.

Haughey, John C. "Church and Kingdom: Ecclesiology in the Light of Eschatology." *Theological Studies* 29 (1968): 72-86.

McBrien, Richard P. *Do We Need the Church?* New York: Harper & Row, 1969.

Niebuhr, H. Richard. *The Kingdom of God in America.* New York: Harper Torch Books, 1959.

*Pannenberg, Wolfhart. *Theology and the Kingdom of God.* Philadelphia: Westminster, 1969.

Perrin, Norman. *The Kingdom of God in the Preaching of Jesus.* Philadelphia: Westminster, 1963.

_____. *Jesus and the Language of the Kingdom.* Philadelphia: Fortress, 1976.

Ruether, Rosemary. *The Radical Kingdom: The Western Experience of Messianic Hope.* New York: Harper & Row, 1970.

Schlink, Edmund. *The Coming Christ and the Coming Church.* Philadelphia: Fortress, 1968.

Schmidt, Karl Ludwig. *Basileia. Bible Key Words from Kittle.* London: A. & C. Black, 1957.

Schnackenburg, Rudolf. "Church and Parousia." In *One, Holy, Catholic, and Apostolic Church,*" pp. 91-134. Edited by Herbert Vorgrimler. New York: Herder & Herder, 1968.

*_____. *God's Rule and Kingdom.* New York: Herder & Herder, 1965.

Skydsgaard, Kristen E. "The Kingdom of God and the Church." *Scottish Journal of Theology* 4 (1951): 383-397.

Stanley, David M. "Kingdom to Church." In *The Apostolic Church in the New Testament,* pp. 5-37. Westminster, Md.: Newman, 1965.

INDEX OF NAMES

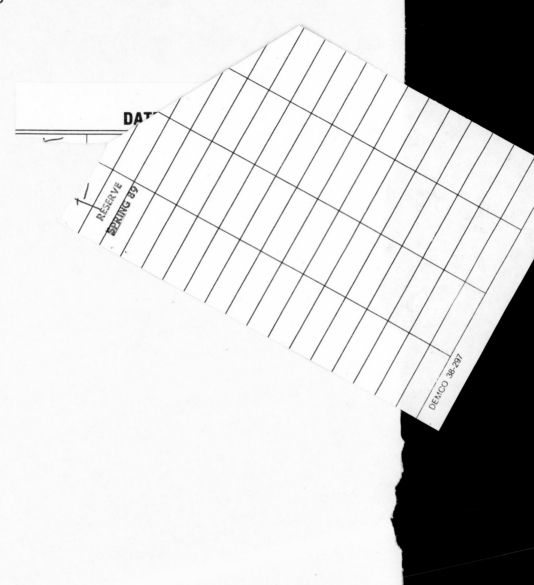